The BADASS COOKBOOK
Awesomely BadAss Recipes

THE BADASS COOKBOOK
Awesomely Badass Recipes

by Daniel Zwicke

The MEAT EATERS ANSWER

to

The THUG KITCHEN COOKBOOK

Daniel Zwicke

YOU DON'T HAVE to BE A BADASS

THE RECIPES ALREADY ARE !

BADASS THAT IS !!!

Broadway Fifth Press
New York, NY
The Bad Ass Cookbook, Most Awesome Recipes Ever
Copyright © 2015 by Daniel Zwicke.

First Edition
First Edition Broadway Fifth Press 2015
New York, New York
Cover Design Daniel Zwicke
Cover photo property of Daniel Zwicke
First Published by Broadway Fifth Press 2015
New York, New York 10014

Library of Congress Cataloging-in-Publication
Data, Zwicke, Daniel
The Bad Ass Cookbook, Most Awesome Recipes Ever

1. Zwicke, Daniel, Cooks – New York (State)—New York—Nonfiction, I Title

ISBN 151715796X
ISBN 978 - 1517157968

The Badass Cookbook

Daniel Zwicke

CONTENTS

CONTENTS

CONTENTS

CONTENTS

11

INTRODUCTION

The Badass Cookbook, guess what? It's Badass! Well not that it's for a Badass or any kind of tough-guy or someone who thinks they're a Badass. No it's just a name, a little joke, we can all use some humor these days. No? Yes a name for a cookbook that contains wonderfully awesome Badass Recipes. Ok, badass is good, one might say supremely good. So if you didn't already know, Badass used in this context means that something is good. Got it?

The collection of recipes are quite interesting in that they are a bit eclectic as a recipe book, however there is a central theme. And the central theme is straightforward, simple, and to the point, that the recipes in the book are simply of America's tastiest most beloved foods of all, and that's it, all the best, and the foods Americans love to eat most. Foods like; Fried Chicken, Barbecued Spare Ribs, Burgers, Chili, Burritos, Hearty Soups, Steak, Eggs, Spaghetti & Meatballs, Meatloaf and what-not.

The recipes here within may be Classic or Secret, some Copycat and what-not, but the common threads are that they have to be Badass Dam Tasty Recipes, America's most loved foods of all, there all here in the Badass Cookbook, the only cookbook of its kind. There's no other.

WINGS & THINGS
Appetizers Wings Things & Finger Foods

Starters, Bar Snacks, and little munchies that aren't main course dishes but things people munch on at cocktail parties, as an appetizer in a multi course meal, or simply while you watching TV at night or whenever. Some of these Wings & Things, snacks and such are some of America's favorite foods. Things like Deviled Eggs, Shrimp Cocktail, Buffalo Chicken Wings, Stuffed Mushrooms, Canapés, and such.

So, we have a few of those kinds of items here, like Danny's famous Honey Mustard Chicken Wings, Devils on Horseback, Chili Cheese Stuffed Mushrooms and such. They're all easy recipes, and you know they're dam tasty. They're Badass. Well? These recipes start the book off and then you're led into all sorts of hearty soups, Fried Chicken, BBQ, Chili, Meatloaf, McRibs, Crab Cakes, and more, they're America's favorite food and you're gonna just love them.

DEVILED EGGS

INGREDIENTS :

8 large Eggs
¼ cup Mayonnaise
2 tablespoons Dijon Mustard
¼ teaspoon Salt
¼ teaspoon ground Black Pepper
1/8 teaspoon Sweet Paprika

Place eggs in a medium sized pot and fill with water to 2" over the eggs. Turn heat on and bring to the boil. Once the water comes to the boil, lower the heat so water is simmering and simmer the eggs for 8 minutes.

Turn heat off and let the eggs sit in the water for 10 minutes. Drain water off eggs, then run cold water over the eggs. Let eggs cool for 15 minutes.

Remove eggs from the water and remove shells from all the eggs.

Cut the eggs in-half lengthwise and remove yolks from the eggs.

Place the yolks in a small mixing bowl. Mash the yolks with the back of a fork. Add salt, pepper, mayonnaise, and mustard to bowl. Mix all ingredients together.

DEVILS on HORSEBACK

If you're having a Cocktail Party with hors d'oeuvres, this is one of the best items to serve. They're real tasty and everyone just loves them.

INGREDIENTS :

24 Dates. Pitted
12 strips Smoked Bacon, cut in-half
6 ounces Blue Cheese (Stilton, Gorgonzola or Maytag Blue)

Make a slit into each date. Stuff a little piece of Blue Cheese into the slit. Repeat until all the dates are stuffed with Blue Cheese.

Wrap a piece of Bacon around each stuffed date. Stick a toothpick through the Bacon and into the center of each stuffed date.

Place on a cookie sheet and bake in a 350 degree oven for 12 – 14 minutes. Remove from oven, and let cool 5 minutes before serving.

CHILI CHEESE STUFFED MUSHROOMS

I invented these Chili Cheese Stuffed Mushrooms one day when I had a little leftover Chili, and I had the idea to stuff some Mushroom Caps with the Chili and top with a little Grated Cheddar. I made them and my guest really like them, and I've been making them ever since, so here's the recipe and I do hope you will enjoy.

INGREDIENTS :

1 pound ground Beef
3 tablespoons Olive Oil
1 medium Onion, peeled and minced fine
2 tablespoons Smoked Paprika
1 tablespoon Tomato Paste
¾ cup water
¼ teaspoon each Kosher Salt & ground Black Pepper

36 medium sized Button Mushrooms
12 ounces grated Cheddar Cheese
¼ cup fresh chopped Parsley (optional)

Place Olive Oil, Beef, and Onions in a large skillet and cook medium heat for 8 minutes. As the beef is cooking, break it up with a wooden spoon.

Add the tomato paste, salt, pepper, Paprika, and water to pan and cook on low heat for 25 minutes, stirring occasionally.

Wash the mushrooms and remove stems from each mushroom. Sprinkle a little Salt & Pepper into the mushrooms to season. Place mushrooms on a cookie pan that has a coating of vegetable oil on it. Place mushrooms in a 350 degree oven and let cook for 12 minutes. Remove from oven. Let cool for 5 minutes.

Fill each Mushroom Cap with a spoonful of Chili, then top each mushroom with grated Cheddar Cheese. Bake in a 350 degree oven until the cheese is nicely melted.

Remove from oven. Let rest for 5 minutes, then sprinkle each mushroom with chopped Parsley. Serve to guests.

SHRIMP COCKTAIL

In my many years of working in the restaurant business and having parties where we passed around hors d'oeuvres at a cocktail parties, some of the food items didn't always go over that well. When it came to serving the Shrimp Cocktail no one refused and they went quickly and people would ask for more. That's the affect of Shrimp Cocktail which is just about everyone's favorite.

INGREDIENTS :

2 pounds Large Shrimp, cleaned
1 tablespoon of Salt, ½ cup Tomato Ketchup
3 tablespoons Prepared Horseradish
8 drops Tabasco sauce or other Hot Sauce Brand

Bring a large pot of salted water to the boil. Add shrimp. Bring back to the boil and once the water comes back to the boil, lower heat to lowest flame and cook for about 4-5 minutes until shrimp are cooked through and you do not see any rawness in the center.

Immediately remove from heat, and drain water off shrimp. Add shrimp to a large bowl of water with ice to stop the cooking, and let them stay for 5 minutes. Drain the shrimp of all water and set to the side.

In a small glass or ceramic bowl, mix the horseradish. Ketchup and Hot Sauce. This is the Cocktail Sauce for the shrimp. Neatly arrange shrimp on a plate or platter and serve with the cocktail sauce in a small bowl.

MARYLAND CRAB CAKES

These Crab Cakes are a great favorite on the East Coast of The United, especially on the Maryland Eastern Shore. They are super easy to make and oh-so tasty. You can make a sandwich out of them or serve as an appetizer or main course, any way you decide is going to be good. I myself love having one as a sandwich.

INGREDIENTS :

1 pound Lump Crab Meat
½ cup Plain Breadcrumbs
4 tablespoons Mayonnaise
1 tablespoon Dijon Mustard
1 large Egg, beaten
½ teaspoon Kosher Salt
½ teaspoon Black Pepper
½ teaspoon Paprika

Place all above ingredient in a large bowl and mix. Divide the mixture into 8 equal portions and form into Crab Cakes.

½ Flour
¼ cup vegetable oil
2 tablespoons Butter

Place the oil and butter in large frying pan that's large enough to hold all of the Crab Cakes, or cook the Crab Cakes in a smaller pan and cook in two batches.

Fry the crab cakes over medium heat until golden brown, about 2 ½ minutes each side. Serve 1 Crab Cake as an appetizer or 2 for a main course with a little salad on the side.

SAUCE: Mix together ½ cup Mayonnaise, 1 tablespoon Dijon Mustard, and 1 tablespoon Ketchup. Place a little dollop on top of each Crab Cake.

BUFFALO CHICKEN WINGS

RECIPE :

2 lbs. Chicken Wings
½ cup vegetable oil, 1/3 stick Margarine or Butter
Black Pepper and Salt
2 ½ tablespoons Hot Sauce (Tabasco, Frank's, etc.)

Prep the wings by cutting off the tip and discarding them, then cut the Wing in half at joint to make 2 pieces.

Season Chicken Wings with Salt & Black Pepper.

Heat vegetable oil in a large frying pan. Cook the Wings in batches, probably 3 batches depending on how many wings you have and how big your pan is.

Cook the wings about 4 minutes on each side over medium heat.

Place the wings in a large baking pan. Set in the oven at 350 degrees for 20 minutes

Melt Butter or Margarine in a small pot.

Remove all oil from pan.

Place Wings in a large bowl with melted butter or margarine and Hot Sauce, mix all thoroughly, coating all the wings.

BLUE CHEESE DIP

1 cup Mayonnaise
4 oz. crumbled Blue Cheese
2 tablespoons White Vinegar, Black Pepper
¼ cup Heavy Cream

In a large bowl, mix all ingredients except Heavy Cream.

Slowly add Heavy Cream mixing with a wooden spoon until dressing is of the consistency you desire.

Slice Celery into 3-inch sticks. Serve Buffalo Wings with Celery Sticks and Blue Cheese Dressing, Abide and Enjoy!

BADASS HONEY MUSTARD WINGS
"They're BadAss Good" !!!

SECRET RECIPE :

2 pounds Chicken Wings
Salt and ground Black Pepper
6 tablespoons Dijon or Brown Mustard
6 tablespoons Canola or Corn Oil
6 Tablespoons Honey, 4 tablespoons Soy Sauce
2 tablespoons Sriracha Thai Sauce or other Garlic
Red Pepper Sauce

Prep the Chicken Wings by cutting off the inedible Tip. The wing is now in a letter "V" shape. Cut in the middle at the joint, cutting the wings into two pieces. Pre heat oven to 400 degrees.

Place all the wings in the largest baking pan you or 2 pans if you don't have one large one to hold all the wings.

Add oil of choice, Salt & Black Pepper to thoroughly coat all the wings with the oil, Salt & Pepper. Cook wings at 400 degrees for 10 minutes. Turn heat down to 350 degrees and continue cooking the wings for about 17 minutes.

Take wings out of oven and add the soy sauce, Honey, Mustard, and Sriracha Sauce to pan with Wings. Mix all ingredients so the Wings get evenly coated.

Put the wings back in oven and cook for seven minutes. Take Wings out of oven. Let cool about 5 minutes. Place on a platter, serve, and Enjoy.

Daniel Zwicke

BADASS GUAC
Guacamole That Is !!!

INGREDIENTS :

1/2 cup finely chopped white onion
2 Jalapeño Peppers, seeded and minced
2 tbsp. finely chopped Fresh Cilantro
Salt, a pinch
2 medium Hass Avocados (ripe)
2 Plum Tomato, chopped to a medium dice

Cut Avocados in half. Remove the pit. Scoop out pulp and put into a medium size glass mixing bowl.

Mash avocado with a potato-masher or back of a wooden spoon to break down the avocado.

Add all remaining ingredients and mix with a wooden spoon.

Serve with Tortilla Chips, and or use as an ingredient for Burritos & Tacos. And Enjoy!

SECRET SALAD DRESSING

Secret Salad Dressing you say? Yes it's Secret, awesome and absolutely Badass. Learn how to make this and you'll be using it for years. It will serve you well and get you lots of compliments. Make it one every couple of weeks or so, keep it in the frig and your all set to go. Pour it over Iceberg, Romaine, Boston Bibb, or any of your favorite lettuce and salad ingredients, this Salad Dressing is killer, so much it part of you arsenal of dishes and your good to go.

INGREDIENTS:

½ Cup Mayonnaise
¼ cup Olive Oil, ¼ Red Wine Vinegar
1 tablespoon water, 1 Garlic Clove, minced fine
¼ teaspoon each of Salt & Black Pepper
¼ teaspoon dry Oregano, ¼ teaspoon dry Basil

Place Mayonnaise and half the Olive Oil in a mixing bowl and mix with a wire-whip. Add remaining Olive Oil, mix again.

Add vinegar a little at a time and mix. Add all remaining ingredients and mix vigorously.

Place whatever lettuce you choose in a large bowl. Add Creamy Italian Dressing, mix and serve.

NOTE: You can make a salad with this tasty dressing with whatever lettuce and other ingredients you choose. Our favorite is Boston Bibb Lettuce with Cucumbers & Tomatoes.

SOUPS

Soups, they are oh-so wonderful! Yes they are. They're tasty, easy to make, and so very affordable. If you're on a budget, there's nothing better than soup to help keep your food expenses down, you just get beat a big pot of soup. And not only do soups help you save money, they help you save time as well. You spend an hour or hour-and-a-half time making a big pot of soup, and once you have it, you well get numerous meals (about 12-14 servings) from that one pot of soup. And after you've made the soup and you want a nice quick meal, all you have do is pull it out of the frig, put some in a small pan, turn on the heat, and Voila, in 5 minutes you got a nice hearty soul satisfy bowl of soup. Our favorites are Lentil, Split Pea, Minestrone, Chicken Noodle, Black Bean, and Manhattan Clam Chowder for a special treat.

If you're just learning how to cook, soups are the way to go into your first forays into cooking and the culinary arts. Soups are extremely easy, and you should have excellent results right from the start, and this will boost your ego and keep you encouraged to go for more. So, here are a few recipes below, dig in, make them, and enjoy.

CHICKEN NOODLE SOUP
a.k.a. Jewish Penicillin

Chicken Noodle Soup, they call it "Jewish Penicillin." It's been known to cure some terrible colds. For sure it will make you fell a whole lot better. But hey, it's not just for eating when you're feeling Under The Weather. No, you can and will eat Chicken Soup any old time at all. This is one of America's favorite, if not the # 1 soup of all. In America that is! So make it and enjoy, and if you ever get a nasty cold, you know what to do.

This is actually two recipes in one, "Almost." In this recipe for Chicken Noodle Soup you will cook a whole chicken. You will use the cooked chicken breast for Chicken Salad and the rest of the chicken, the legs and thighs will go into the soup. That's awesome Dude!!!

Ingredients:

1 whole roasting Chicken 4-5 pounds
2 medium Onions cut into a medium dice
5 whole cloves of garlic, Peeled
6 stalks of Celery cut into large cube
6 Carrots cut into a large dice
6 quarts of water
1 pound package of Egg Noodles
1 Bay Leaf, 1 teaspoon Salt
½ teaspoon Black Pepper

Cooking Procedures:

Fill a large 8 qt. Pot with water. Wash the chicken and place it into the pot. Cover the pot. Turn on the flame and bring the water to the boil. Once the water reaches the boiling point, lower the flame so the water simmers at a slow simmer.

Add the carrots, celery, garlic, onions, Bay Leaf, salt, and pepper to the pot.

Let the soup simmer for 1 hour and 15 minutes.

Remove the chicken from the pot and let it cool down.

While the chicken is cooling, cook the Egg Noodles according to the directions on the package. Drain the noodles, then sprinkle with a little olive oil so the noodles won't stick together.

Once the chicken has cooled down, remove the breast and reserve to make chicken salad with.

Pick all the rest of the meat off the chicken bones and put into the soup pot. Let the chicken meat simmer in the pot for ten minutes. Add the noodles and let simmer for 2 minutes. The soup is now ready to serve.

NOTE: If you'd like you can substitute rice for the noodles to make Chicken and Rice Soup. To do so, cook one cup of rice in 2 ½ cups water for 15 minutes and drain. At the point where you take the chicken out of the pot, you will put the rice into the pot of soup and let simmer 5 minutes.

SPLIT PEA SOUP

Split Pea Soup, "It's as American as Apple Pie." Well not really, but not far off the mark, it's that popular, an American favorite. It's real easy to make, and doesn't require many ingredients. Split Peas is like mostly all soup Soul Satisfying and quite inexpensive for the budget minded. What more can you ask for I ask?

INGREDIENTS :

1 medium Onion, peeled and finely Diced
1 ½ tablespoons Vegetable Oil (Canola,
Corn Oil, etc.)
1 Carrot peeled and cut to medium dice
1 Russet or Idaho Potato, peel and cut to medium dice
(Optional)
1 pound bag of dry Split Peas
¼ pound Ham, diced
Salt and Black Pepper to taste

Place oil and onions in a 6-quart pot. Cook over medium heat for 2 minutes. Add ham and sauté for 2 minutes. Add all remaining ingredients to pot.

Add enough water to cover 1 inch past all ingredients. Bring up to the boil over high heat. When ingredients come to the boil, lower heat to low. Cook for about 1 hour and 15 minutes, stirring occasionally and making sure to keep soup at a low simmer. The soup is done when all the Split Peas have liquefied. Serve with Croutons or Bread. Save remaining soup in frig.

MANHATTAN CLAM CHOWDER
The Classic Recipe

What the hell happened to the Clam Chowder? When I was a kid growing up in the 60's & 70's New York Metro Area, Manhattan Clam Chowder was everywhere. Lots of restaurants and diners had it on the menu, and it would pop up at church and local firehouse functions. Manhattan Clam Chowder, you hardly ever see it anymore, I don't know why, it's dam tasty, easy to make, and real healthy too, with the clams and tons of vegetables in it. So what happened? Guess it got passé and out-of-favor with some, but no matter, it's still the great soup it's always been, many will agree. So whether you've never had it, or you haven't had it for some time, give it a shot, its awesomely Badass, I'm sure you'll agree.

INGREDIENTS :

12 Quahog Clams (Chowder Clams) washed
4 slices of Bacon cut into ¼" dice
1 medium Onion diced
2 stalks of Celery, diced
2 Carrots, peeled and cut to medium dice
1 Green Bell Pepper, seeded and diced
1 small Bottle of Clam Juice
3 large Idaho Potatoes, peeled and diced
1 28 can whole Tomatoes roughly chopped
6 cups of water, 1 Bay Leaf
¼ teaspoon Thyme, Salt & Black Pepper

Place clams in a large 8 Qt. size pot. Add 1 ½ cups water.

Cover the pot with a lid. Turn heat on to a high flame and cook until all the clam shells have opened, about 6 minutes.

Turn off heat. Place clams with the cooking liquid in a large bowl. Let cool.

Rinse the pot with water and place back on the stove.

Turn heat on to medium and add the Bacon and cook for about 4 to 5 minutes, stirring with a wooden spoon. The Bacon will render its fat. Remove half the fat from the pot and discard.

Add Onion and Green Pepper, sauté for 4 minutes. Add Celery, Carrots, water, tomatoes, and potatoes. Turn heat up to high and bring to the boil. As soon as contents comes the boil, lower the heat so contents is at a medium simmer.

Add bay Leaf, Thyme, Salt & Pepper to taste. Simmer for 25 minutes.

While the soup is simmering, remove the Clams from their shell. Chop the clams into ¼" dice.

After the soup has simmered, add the chopped Clams and clam cooking liquid. Simmer for 4 minutes over very low heat. Serve as is or with Oyster Crackers.

NOTE : If you don't eat meat, you can omit the Bacon.

PORTUGUESE KALE & POTATO SOUP

This is a wonderful ethnic soup from Portugal that they know quite well up in New England whether someone is Portuguese or not. the soup is absolutely awesome! No doubt you'll agree. If you've never had it before, please give it a try, we know you'll just love it. Enjoy!

8 tablespoons Olive Oil
12 ounces Linguica Sausage (Smoked Portuguese Sausage)
or Kielbasa (Smoke polish Sausage)
1 medium Onion, peeled and chopped
4 cloves Garlic, peeled and sliced
1 ½ pounds Baking Potatoes, peeled and cut to ¾" dice
1 pound Kale, wash, remove stems and sliced
½ teaspoon each of Salt & Black Pepper, 7 cups water

Cut whatever sausage you are using into 1/3" slices. Put olive oil and Sausage in a large pot and cook on low-medium heat until the sausages are slightly brown, about 5 minutes. Remove sausages from pot with a slotted spoon and place in a bowl until later.

Add Onion to pot and cook on low heat for 6 minutes. Add Garlic and cook for 2 minutes. Add water, potatoes, salt, & Black Pepper to pot and cook on a medium simmer for 20 minutes. Remove 1/3 of the potatoes and mash in a bowl. Put these mashed potatoes back in the pot. Add Kale and cook for 8 minutes on medium heat. Add sausages back to soup and cook on low heat for 6 minutes. Turn heat off, the soup is ready to serve.

CUBAN BLACK BEAN SOUP

INGREDIENTS :

1 pound dry Black Beans
¼ cup Olive Oil
1 large Onion, peeled and chopped fine
1 Green Bell Pepper, seeded and chopped
6 Garlic cloves, peeled and minced
1 Ham Hock
1 teaspoon Cumin
1 teaspoon Kosher Salt
1 teaspoon ground Black Pepper
2 Bay Leaves

GARNISH :

Sour Cream
Chopped Scallions

Put the dry beans in a large bowl and pick through for any stones that might be in the beans. Wash the beans three times. Put the beans in the bowl and cover with water by 2 inches.

Take beans out of the refrigerator and drain in a colander. Wash the beans and leave in the colander

Place a large pot on top of the stove. Put the Olive Oil and Green Peppers in the pot and cook for 10 minutes on low heat.
Add the onions to the pot and cook on medium heat for 5 minutes. Add the garlic, salt, Cumin, and Black

Pepper and cook on low heat for two minutes while stirring with a wooden spoon.

Add the Beans to the pot and cover with water bring the water to 2 inches past the beans. Add Ham Hock and Bay Leaves.

Cook the beans in for 2 hours low heat. Make sure to stir the soup occasionally to keep the soup from sticking on the bottom. After cooking for about 2 hours the beans should be tender yet slightly firm.

Remove 1/3 of the beans and pass through a food mill to mash the beans. Put the mashed beans back in the soup and cook on low heat for 10 minutes while stirring.

The soup is ready to serve. Place in bowls and add a little dollop of Sour Cream and chopped Scallions on top.

NEW ORLEANS CREOLE GUMBO

If you've ever been down to one of my favorite cities in the World, The Big Easy, New Orleans, then you've no doubt had a bowl of Gumbo or two. They say New Orleans as a city itself is *One Big Gumbo*, a Gumbo of People Food, Culture, and Jazz, that's New Orleans. A Gumbo is a mixture of foods, you can throw anything in a Gumbo? Well almost anything. A basic Gumbo is usually made with Chicken, Vegetables (The Trinity), and Andouille Sausage, and from here you can add; Shrimp, Crab Meat, Oysters, or any Seafood you like, or simply just eat the wonderful Gumbo of Chicken & Sausage alone. Rabbit Gumbo is quite popular, and there's Duck Gumbo too. So, if you've been to New Orleans, and you've had Gumbo, no doubt you crave it every now and then. So if you can't get down there to get a bowl, and you want one, well here you go, we've got a real good recipe below. Get some friends together, make the Gumbo and do like they do in New Orleans, "Let The Good Times Roll!"

INGREDIENTS :

3 /12 pounds Chicken Thighs
1 pound Andouille Sausage, sliced 1/2" thick (or Kielbasa)
1 tablespoon Creole Seasoning (we like Tony Chaceree's)
½ cup Vegetable Oil, 1 cup Flour
1 large Spanish Onion, peeled and chopped

4 stalks Celery, washed and chopped
2 medium Green Bell Peppers, seeded and chopped
1 teaspoon Kosher Salt
½ teaspoon Cayenne Pepper
½ teaspoon dried Thyme
2 Bay Leaves
4 cups chicken broth
4 ½ cups water
4 tablespoons Tomato Paste
2 pounds Shrimp, shelled and deveined
½ pound Okra, wash and cut in 4 pieces each
½ cup Scallions, wash and chopped

4 cups Boiled Rice

Place 4 tablespoons of the oil in a large 8-quart pot with the Sausage and cook on low heat for 7 minutes. Remove the sausage from the pan with a slotted spoon, leaving the fat in the pan. Set sausage on the side.

Season the Chicken Thighs with the Creole Seasoning and fry in the pot over medium heat, until the chicken is nice and golden brown, about 3 ½ minutes each side.

Remove the chicken from pot with thongs or a slotted spoon and set aside.

Add the remaining oil to pan and turn heat on to low. Add the flour and mix with a wire whip while cooking and stirring. Cook for 12-15 minutes until you get a nice brown color. Be careful not to burn.

Add the onions, celery, and Bell Pepper to the pot with the Thyme, Cayenne, Black Pepper, and 1 teaspoon of the Creole Seasoning. Stir with a wooden spoon while cooking for 6 minutes.

Place the Chicken Broth & water in a small pot and bring to the boil.

Add 1 cup of the hot chicken broth to the pot with roux and vegetables and stir. Cook on medium heat to minutes. Add remaining chicken broth and Tomato Paste and cook as you stir for 5 minutes, then let this simmer at low heat for 15 minutes.

Add the Andouille Sausage, the Chicken Thighs, Okra, and the Bay Leaves and cook on a low to medium simmer for 45 minutes.

Add the Shrimp to the pot and cook on low heat for 6 minutes. Turn the heat off. Your Gumbo is done and ready to go.

Cook 8 ounces of Long Grain Rice according to the direction on the package.

Once the rice is cooked, place some in a coffee cup and press the rice into the cup so it takes its shape. Invert the cup of rice into a shallow soup bowl so you have a nice cup-shaped mound of rice in the bowl. Spoon Gumbo into the bowl and top with fresh chopped Scallions

NOTE : Gumbo is eat either in a smaller portion for a starter or soup course, or a larger portion in the form of a main course with rice.

BADASS BBQ SAUCE
It's Bad Ass as The Name Implies

This Sauce is awesome! It's Badass! It's got Bourbon! Put it on Chicken, your Barbecued Ribs, on Burgers, make a Badass BBQ Duck, your gonna love it. It's Danny's Badass BBQ Sauce, and it makes everything better, we're sure you'll agree.

The SECRET RECIPE:

3 tablespoons Butter, 2 ½ cups Ketchup
1 medium Onions, peeled and minced fine
3 ounces Kentucky Bourbon (Makers Mark, Jim Beam)
4 tablespoons Dark Molasses, 3 TBS. Brown Sugar
2 tablespoons Dijon or Brown Mustard
Juice and Zest from 1 large Navel Orange
6 tablespoons Lea & Perrin's Worcestershire Sauce
1 tablespoon Garlic Powder, 2 teaspoons Kosher Salt
3 teaspoon Black Pepper, 2 teaspoon Cayenne Pepper

Place onions and butter in a small pan. Turn heat to a low flame and cook the onions for 8 minutes. Add Bourbon and turn heat to high. Cook for 3 minutes on high heat.

Add Brown sugar and cook on low heat for 2 minutes while stirring. Add all remaining ingredients. Turn heat to a low fame and cook for 25 minutes on very low heat, stirring occasionally. If the sauce gets to thick, add a little water and continue cooking. After 25 minutes, remove from heat. The sauce is ready.

BADASS RIBS

Barbecue Spare Ribs, who doesn't love them? No one I tell you. Well, maybe not vegetarians, or someone who's out of their mind. You'd have to be not to love these tasty suckers, Pork Spare Ribs with Badass Bourbon BBQ Sauce, it's doesn't get any better than this Boys & Girls. The recipe follows, so "Go for it!"

INGREDIENTS:

1 – 4 pound rack of Pork Spare Ribs
Kosher Salt & Black Pepper to taste
1 teaspoon Smoked Paprika
Bad Ass BBQ Sauce

UNTENSILS :

1 Wire Roasting Rack
1 Baking Pan
Aluminum Foil

Pre-heat oven to 400 degrees.

Season the ribs on both sides with Salt & Black Pepper. Sprinkle Smoke Paprika on both sides of the Ribs. Rub the Salt, Paprika, and Black Pepper into the ribs with your hands.

Place the Wire Roasting Rack in the Roasting Pan and place the Ribs on top of the rack. Place in the oven and let the ribs cook at 400 degrees for 15 minutes.
Lower heat to 350 degrees and cook for 30 minutes.

Remove pan from stove and let cool down a few minutes. Turn the heat in the oven down to 300 degrees. Once the pan is cool enough to handle, cover and close tightly with aluminum foil.

Put Ribs back in oven and let cook at 300 degrees for 1 hour and 30 minutes.

Remove pan from oven. Take aluminum foil off of pan. Brush the ribs with the BBQ Sauce. Put back in the oven and let cook at 300 degrees for 15 minutes.

Remove ribs from the oven and let rest 10 minutes before serving. Cut the ribs between the bones and serve 3 to 4 ribs per person. Serve with your favorite side dishes and enjoy yourself, "You're in Hog Heaven," and there's nothing better.

NOTE : This recipe is for making Bad Ass BBQ Ribs made with Badass BBQ Sauce on page 44, but you can cook the ribs using whatever sauce you like, including one of the other sauces in this book. What is also very good, is the ribs cooked without any sauce, you can simply just season and rub the ribs with Salt, Black, and Smoked Paprika and cook in the oven as described above, and don't put any sauce on at all. Believe be, they taste dam good this way, and you should definitely try them this way some time. And you can always serve a little BBQ Sauce on the side, for anyone who wants to dip in and Enjoy!

BONE SUCKING BBQ SAUCE
"It's Bone Sucking Good" !!!

SECRET INGREDIENTS :

2 cups Ketchup
¾ cup water
3 tablespoons Apple Cider Vinegar
½ teaspoon Garlic Powder
½ Teaspoon Onion Powder
3 teaspoons Dry Mustard
5 tablespoons Brown Sugar
5 tablespoons Molasses
½ teaspoon Liquid Smoke

Place all ingredients in a medium size pot and stir. Cook on very low heat for 20 to 30 minutes, stirring occasionally to keep sauce from burning.

Remove from heat and let sauce cool. Slather this sauce on Chicken or Ribs for Bone Sucking-ly Good BBQ-ed Chicken or Ribs. Or make a Bone Sucking BBQ Burger by cooking up a nice Hamburger that's slather with this sauce for a Bone Sucking BBQ Hamburger. What's better than that? Well, the Ribs probably.

BARBECUED CHICKEN
with Badass BBQ Sauce

INGREDIENTS :

1 small Broiler Chicken, split in half, 1/3 teaspoon Kosher Salt
½ teaspoon ground Black Pepper
½ teaspoon Paprika
1/3 cup Bad Ass Barbecue Sauce (or your favorite sauce)
4 tablespoons Olive Oil

Pre-heat oven to 400 degrees. Place the oil and the chicken skin side down on a baking pan. Season the chicken side facing up with half the salt, pepper, and Paprika. Turn the chicken over and season the skin-side of the Chicken with the remaining salt, pepper, and Paprika.

Place Chicken in oven with skin side down, and cook the Chicken for 15 minutes at 400 degrees. Lower heat to 350. Turn the chicken over so the skin side is down Brush half the Barbecue Sauce on Chicken, and cook at 350 degrees for 12 minutes.

Turn chicken over so skin side is up. Brush Barbecue Sauce on the skin side of the Chicken and cook for 12 minutes at 350 degrees. Remove Chicken from oven and let rest before serving. Sever with Mac & Cheese, Cole Slaw, Baked Potatoes or whatever you like.

NOTE : Instead of making this BBQ Chicken with a whole Chicken, you can make it with just Chicken Thighs (my favorite), or just Legs & Thighs when they're on sale, it's all up to you.

FINGER LICKIN GOOD FRIED CHICKEN
The Colonel's Finger Lickin Good Fried Chicken

Yes it's Finger Lickin Good, we're sure you'll agree. This Chicken taste just like the Colonel's KFC Secret Recipe, eaten by hundreds of millions of people over the years, it's that dam good. In fact, they're Badass as can be!

SECRET RECIPE :

7 cups of Water
¼ cup of Kosher Salt, 4 tablespoons Sugar
2 tablespoons Black Pepper

Mix Salt, Sugar, and Black Pepper into the water, This is a brine that you will put the chicken in.

1 - 3 pound Chicken cut into 8 pieces

Add the chicken to the water brine in a large bowl or pot. Put into eh refrigerator for at least 2 hours before cooking. If you can do this over night it would be even better, but not absolutely necessary.

NOTE: You can skip the brining step if you'd like. Your chicken will still taste very good, but?

2 large Eggs and 1 cup of Milk
1 teaspoon of Salt and 1 teaspoon Black Pepper

Beat the Eggs. Add the milk, salt and pepper and mix. Set aside until later.

SECRET 11 HERBS & SPICES

1 ½ cups All Purpose Flour
1 teaspoon dry Oregano
1 teaspoon ground Sage
1 teaspoon dry Basil
1 teaspoon Cayenne Pepper
1 teaspoon Sugar, 1 teaspoon Salt
1 teaspoon Black Pepper, 2 teaspoons Sweet Paprika
½ teaspoon ground Cumin
1 teaspoon Onion Powder, 1 teaspoon Garlic Powder

Mix all the above ingredients thoroughly in a large bowl. Remove the Chicken from the brine and set in a colander or wire rack to let the brine drain off.

One by one, dredge each piece of chicken in the Flour-Herb mixture. Shake off excess flour. Next dredge each piece of chicken into the egg-mixture, shaking off excess egg, then placing the egg coated chicken back into the flour mixture. Shake off excess flour from chicken and place on a plate to rest.

While chicken is resting, place 5 inches of vegetable oil, lard or Cisco in a small pot. Heat the Oil on a high flame. Once the oil is hot enough, place four pieces of chicken in the hot oil and until chicken is cooked through and golden brown, about 12 minutes.

Remove the chicken from the hot oil and set aside. Place remaining 4 pieces of chicken in the hot oil and cook for 12 minutes, until done. Serve with whatever side dishes you like and enjoy.

BADASS FRIED CHICKEN

RECIPE :

1 small Broiler Chicken, cut into 8 pieces
7 cups of Water
¼ cup of Kosher Salt, 4 tablespoons Sugar
2 tablespoons Black Pepper

Put all the above ingredients in a large bowl or pot and mix and let the chicken brine in this over night.

2 cups All Purpose Flour
1 tablespoon Paprika, 1 teaspoon Garlic Powder
1 teaspoon Cayenne Pepper, 1 teaspoon Kosher Salt
1 teaspoon ground Black Pepper

Place flour and all the above seasonings in a large bowl and mix. Remove chicken from the brine, shake off excess water and pat-dry the chicken with Paper Towels.

Get a heavy bottom skillet and put either Peanut or Canola Oil in to make a 2" depth of oil. Turn heat on to high and get the oil hot enough for frying.

Place the chicken one piece at a time into the flour and mix to coat chicken with seasoned flour. Shake off excess flour and place each piece of chicken in hot oil to fry.

Cook the chicken until golden brown and the chicken is cooked through, about 10-12 minutes, turning the chicken occasionally.

CHICKEN FRIED STEAK

Chicken Fried Steak is without question one of the South's favorite dishes. It's much loved and 2nd only to Barbecued Whatever and Fried Chicken. Make it, make some Mashed Potatoes and Biscuits to go with it and you're sure to be in 7th Heaven. Enjoy!

INGREDIENTS :

2 Sirloin Steaks, cut ½" thick
2 Eggs beaten with ½ cup of Milk

Place milk & eggs and a pinch of Salt & Black Pepper in a shallow bowl and mix.

1 ½ cups Flour
½ teaspoon each of Salt, Back Pepper, and Paprika

Mix flour in a bowl with Salt, Pepper, and Paprika.

Season both sides of the steak with Salt & Black Pepper.

Dredge both sides of each steak in the seasoned flour and shake off excess flour. Place the steaks in bowl with the eggs.

Fill a large skillet with 1 cup of Canola or other vegetable oil and heat the oil to 350 degrees.

Remove the steaks one-by-one from the eggs and shake off excess egg. Then dredge the steak back in seasoned four. Do this to both steaks. Then add the steaks to the hot oil and fry until both sides of the steaks are golden brown, about 4 minutes per side. Turn the heat off.

Remove steaks from the pan and set atop clean paper towels. Pour off all but about 5 tablespoons of the oil in the pan. Add 3 tablespoons of flour to the pan and whisk with a wire whip, cooking over low heat, stirring constantly.

Slowly add 1 ¾ cups of Milk to the pan as you stir constantly and cook over low-medium heat for 5-6 minutes. Add ½ teaspoon of Black Pepper to the gravy and mix.

Serve each person a steak on a plate and pour the gravy over the Chicken Fried Steak. If you like serve with Mashed Potatoes and Biscuits (Biscuit recipe follows). Enjoy!

EASY DROP BISCUITS
"They're Just Yummy" !!!!

INGREDIENTS :

3 cups All Purpose Flour
4 teaspoons Baking Powder
2 teaspoons Kosher Salt
1 ½ cups Milk
8 ounces (2 Sticks) Unsalted Butter, cut into cubes & chilled

In a large bowl, mix together the Salt, Flour, and Baking Powder.

Place Butter in the bowl with the Flour and with a Pastry Blender (or Fork) until the Flour & Butter resemble course meal. (If you have a Food Processor, you can do this step in it).

Add Milk and mix by hand until all comes together in a wet slightly stick mix. Heat oven to 375 degrees.

Grease a cookie pan with butter. Using a Large Ice Cream Scoop or a ¼ Cup Measuring Cup, scoop dough out of bowl and on to the greased cookie sheet one-by-one.

Place in oven and bake until golden brown and cooked through, about 18 minutes. Serve with your Fried Chicken and enjoy the heck out of them.

CORN BREAD

INGREDIENTS :

1 cup Yellow Corn Meal, ¾ cup All Purpose Flour
1 tablespoon Sugar, ¼ teaspoon Salt
1 ½ teaspoons Baking Powder
½ teaspoon Baking Soda
6 tablespoons Butter, melted
2 Eggs, 1 ½ cups Buttermilk

Place the Corn Meal, Flour, Baking Powder, Baking Soda, and Salt in a large glass mixing bowl and mix thoroughly.

In a separate bowl mix together the Eggs, Buttermilk, and Butter.

Heat oven to 350 degrees. Butter a 8" X 8" glass baking pan.

Pour the wet ingredients into the bowl with the dry ingredients and gently mix with a spatula or wooden spoon until all the ingredients are completely mixed.

Pour the batter into the buttered baking pan and place in the oven. Cook until the top is golden brown and when you stick a toothpick into the Corn Bread it comes out clean, about 25-30 minutes. Remove from oven and let cool 10 minutes before serving.

NOTE : To make Jalapeno Corn Bread, de-seed 3 Jalapeno Peppers, mince and mix into the Corn Bread Batter and bake.

BEST POTATO SALAD EVER
"It's Badass!"

Man, there's nothing quite like Potato Salad, I just love it. I love it so much that when my Dad would take us to a diner to get Cheeseburgers, I'd always ask if I could get Potato Salad instead of the Fries. They'd always oblige me and I was always happy eating my Burger with Potato Salad instead of French Fries, with my Coca-Cola. "Ah, the good old days." This Potato Salad is really awesome with some Ribs or Barbecued Chicken. The contrast of the hot Chicken and its tangy Barbecue Sauce is awesome against the cool coldness of the mayonnaise dressed potatoes with scallions and the seasoning is one of the World's most underrated culinary pairings of all. Well, you're reading this and you know of this little secret, so go ahead and give it a try, you'll be glad you did, it's friggin awesome and this is The Best Potato Salad Ever! Tell all your friends!

INGREDIENTS :

6 large Baking Potatoes
2 Celery stalks, washed
6 Scallions, washed, dried and chopped
4 hard Boiled Eggs, peeled
2 tablespoons White Vinegar
1 & ¾ cups Real Mayonnaise
1 tablespoon Mustard, ¾ teaspoon Celery Seed
½ teaspoon each of Kosher Salt & Black Pepper
½ teaspoon Sweet Paprika

Peel the potatoes and cut into quarters. Place the potatoes in a pot and fill with water. Put 1 teaspoon of Salt in the water and cook potatoes with the water boiling until the potatoes when pierced with a fork are tender to the touch, about 12-14 minutes. Once cooked, drain the potatoes in a colander, shake off excess water and let sit in the colander to cool for 15 minutes.

Once the potatoes have cooled, dice into large diced pieces and place in a large glass or ceramic mixing bowl. Add the vinegar to the bowl and mix with the potatoes, and let the potatoes marinate in the vinegar for 10 minutes.

Add the Salt, Black Pepper, and Celery Seeds to the bowl and mix. Chop the Hard Boiled Eggs, add to the bowl and mix with potatoes.

Add the Mustard and Scallions and mix. Add the Mayonnaise and mix to fully incorporated. Sprinkle the Paprika over the Potato Salad, cover with plastic wrap and chill in the refrigerator for a at least 1 hour before serving. Serve with Burgers, Barbecued Chicken or Ribs, with sandwiches or whatever you like.

A crazy idea that's Crazy Good. Make some Cowboy Chili and this potato salad at the same time. Put a big scoop of the *Best Potato Salad Ever* in the middle of the bowl, then fill the bowl with Chili. Yes it sound Crazy, but it works. You'll be amazed how dam good it is, with the contrast of the rich hot beef chili against cool creamy lushness of the Potato Salad. It's *da Bomb*, and you know it's Badass as can be.

COWBOY CHILI

This is a great Chili recipe. It's real easy to make and quite versatile too. Eat it in a Bowl with chopped raw onion and Cheddar Cheese on top, inside Burritos or Tacos or in the Cincinnati Favorite 3-Wat Chili over Spaghetti, it's all good.

INGREDIENTS:

3 pounds ground Beef (Chuck is preferred)
4 medium Onions, cut into a medium dice
8 cloves of Garlic, peeled and minced
1-28 ounce can crushed Tomato
1 cup water
1 teaspoon Salt
2 tablespoons Cumin, 1 tablespoon Oregano
2 tablespoons Sweet Paprika
1 teaspoon Cayenne Pepper
1-2 teaspoons Hot Sauce (Tabasco or what you like)
1 tablespoon Lea & Perrin's Worcestershire Sauce

Get a large 6-8 quart pot and line the bottom with vegetable oil. Turn the flame to medium heat.

Add ground chop meat and cook for about 12 minutes until the meat loses its raw color. Turn off heat.

Put the meat in a colander to drain excess fat. In the same large pot, add the onions and cook over medium heat for 5 minutes. Add the garlic cook for 3 minutes.
Add the ground meat back to the pot. Sprinkle the Salt and Black Pepper onto the Beef and sauté for 2 minutes.

Add the tomatoes, oregano, Paprika, and Cumin. Turn the flame up to high until the ingredients start to bubble, lower the flame so the Chili will cook at a gentle simmer. Let simmer for 1 hour.

Add the Hot Sauce and Worcestershire Sauce and continue simmering the Chili for another ½ hour. The CHILI is now finished and ready to eat on its own or with a couple crushed Saltine Crackers, with rice and beans as Chili con Carne, or to make into Burritos or Tacos, or even a most outstanding Chili Dog. "Enjoy!"

If you want the Chili hotter, you can increase the amount of Cayenne and Tabasco or other Hot Sauce. In this recipe we make it so you can just start to discern that it is just slightly hot, but not really too hot. This is the way some like it. If you want to make it hotter, you can at any time. But once you pot hot peppers in you can't take them out.

CHUNKY CHILI
North Carolina Style

Some prefer their Chili chunky style. If you do, this one's for you. Like most chili recipes, it's real easy to make. The key to making it extra tasty is to make sure that when you brown the meat, make sure that you get a good golden brown color on the meat, which will help give the Chili and extra layer of Beef flavor.

You can serve this Chili, Chili con Carne Style with rice, inside Tacos or Burritos, or simply as a Bowl of Chili with chopped raw onion and grated Cheddar on top. It's a winner, so enjoy.

RECIPE :

3 pounds Beef Chuck cut into 1 - inch cubes
8 tablespoons Vegetable Oil (Canola, Corn Oil etc.)
1 cup water
1 large Onion, peeled and chopped fine
8 cloves Garlic, peeled and chopped fine
1 6 ounce can Tomato Paste
1 tablespoon Sweet Paprika
1 teaspoon Cumin
2 tablespoons Cayenne Pepper
3 tablespoons Worcestershire Sauce (Lea & Perrin's)
1 teaspoon Black Pepper
1 teaspoon Kosher Salt
1 – 14 ounce can Red Kidney Beans (optional)

Season beef with a little Slat & Black Pepper. Place oil and beef in 6-8 quart pot. Brown the beef in two separate batches until all the beef has a nice golden brown color. Remove all the browned beef from pan and set aside.

Add ¼ of the water to the pan and turn heat on high. Scrape the bottom of the pan with a wooden spoon to release the brown bits that stick to the pan after browning the beef. There's a lot of flavor in those little brown bits, believe it or not, and they help give the Chili a nice rich beef flavor. Cook on high-heat scraping the bottom of the pan until the water is reduce by half. By the way, this process is known as deglazing, and you will do this anytime you are braising meat or making a stew.

Put the browned beef back in the pan, and all of the remaining ingredients except the Kidney Beans.

Bring everything up to the boil. Once all has come up to the boil, lower the heat to a very low flame and cook until the beef is nice and tender, about 2 hours.

Serve each person a bowl of this Chunky Chili as is or with chopped raw onions and grated Cheddar Cheese on the side, and whatever other condiments you like to serve with your Chili. Enjoy!

CHILI For a CROWD ... "It'll Feed 60!"

Got a crowd of people to feed, but not a ton of money? This is the recipe for you. This tasty Chili recipe will easily feed 50 – 60 people. And it doesn't require a lot of work, especially since you're feeding a large crowd. If you want to spread this chili even further you can cook some rice and serve it with boiled rice. A favorite down in Cincinnati know as Three Way Chili will stretch it even further as you serve the Chili over cooked spaghetti with Cheddar Cheese on top, though the extra cheese will bring your cost up, it's cheaper to serve it in a bowl. Cost will matter to some, others it won't. No matter, this is a wonderful recipe on three fronts; it's cheap, oh-so easy to make, and tasty to boot. Enjoy!

INGREDIENTS :

7 ½ pounds Ground Beef (20% fat to 80% lean ratio)
¼ cup Vegetable Oil (Corn, Canola, etc.)
3 large Spanish Onions, peeled and chopped
20 cloves Garlic, peeled and minced
2 – 4 oz. cans chopped Green Chili Peppers (drained)
5 – 28 ounce cans Crushed Tomatoes
4 – 28 ounce cans Tomato Puree
1 – 6 ounce can Tomato Paste
3 tablespoons Kosher Salt
1 quart of water or more as needed
8 tablespoons ground Cumin

8 tablespoons Black Pepper
7 tablespoons Chili Powder
3 tablespoons Smoked Paprika
5-6 cans Kidney Beans, drained and washed with water

Get a large 16 quart pot to cook the Chili in. Add half the oil to the pot with the onions and cook on low heat for 8 minutes. Add garlic and continue cooking on low heat for 3 minutes. Season with a little salt & Black Pepper and mix. Turn heat off.

Get a large frying pan to brown the beef in. Take some of the beef and place in frying pan with a little oil and cook on medium heat until the beef loses all raw color. Season each batch of beef with a little salt & Black Pepper as you cook it. Make sure to break up the beef with a wooden spoon and stir as you're cooking.

You will be browning the beef in several batches in the large frying pan, then adding each batch of browned ground beef into the large pot.

Once all the beef has been browned and is in the big pot, place all remaining ingredients in the pot, except for the Kidney Beans which will go in the pot for the last 15 minutes of cooking the Chili.

Cook the Chili on a low to medium simmer for 1 hour and thirty minutes. Make sure to stir and get the wooden spoon on the bottom of the pot as you stir to keep the Chili from burning on the bottom. You don't won't to ruin a whole big pot of Chili by burning it, so make sure you do this every 7 minutes or so.

After the Chili has been cooking for 1 hour and 15 minutes, add the Kidney Beans and continue cooking for 15 minutes more.

Your Chili is now finished. Let it set for 15 minutes before serving. Serve with chopped un-cooked onions or Scallions to go on top of each bowl of Chili along with grated Cheddar Cheese.

CINCINNATI 3 WAY CHILI

Cincinnati 3 Way Chili is a phenomenon of the mid-western city of Cincinnati, Ohio. After the great state of Texas, the folks around Cincinnati are probably America's second biggest fans and eaters of Chili, and they do it in a very special way, known as 3 Way Chili.

INGREDIENTS :

1 ½ pounds lean Ground Beef
1 large Onion, peeled and chopped fine
7 tablespoons Olive Oil
3 cloves Garlic, peeled and minced
½ teaspoon Allspice, ½ teaspoon Cinnamon
½ teaspoon Cayenne Pepper, ½ teaspoon Paprika
1 ½ teaspoons Cocoa Powder
1 ½ teaspoons Cider Vinegar, ¾ cup water
1 – 15 ounce can Tomato Sauce (Tomato Puree)
½ teaspoon each of Salt & Black Pepper

Place olive oil and onions in a large skillet. Turn heat on and cook onions over medium heat for 5 minutes. Add the Ground Beef, Garlic, Salt & Black Pepper and cook on medium heat until the beef loses its raw color, about 5 minutes. Add all the remaining ingredient, turn heat up to high and bring to the boil. Once everything has come up to the boil, lower the heat and simmer on a low-medium simmer for 1 hour and 30 minutes. Turn the heat off.

The WAYS of CINCINNATI CHILI

A "way" in Cincinnati Chili lingo represents one ingredient for one-way, and here are the *Ways* below.

3-WAYS Spaghetti + Chili + Cheese

4-WAYS Spaghetti + Chili + Cheese + Onions or Beans

5-WAYS Spaghetti + Chili + Cheese + Onions + Beans

To make 3 WAY CHILI, cook 1 pound of Spaghetti according to the directions on the package. Once finished cooking, drain the spaghetti in a colander and shake off excess water.

Plate the Spaghetti evenly among 4 plates. Top the Spaghetti with a cup of your Cincinnati Chili., and top the Chili with shredded Cheddar are American Cheese.

If you want 4 or 5 WAY CHILI, just chop some raw onion and put it on top of the Chili, and for 5 Way Chili, add chopped raw onion and Beans.

NOTE : For the Beans, drain and wash the beans of a 15 oz. can of Kidney Beans, add to a pot and heat with ¼ cup of water for 5 minutes.

TACOS & BURRITOS

Tacos and Burritos, Americans just love them. They've become a part of everyday American eating whether you make them at home or get them at a Mexican or Tex-Mex restaurant, Taco Truck, or Taco stand. But dam, ever notice that the tacos are real tiny and not all that substantial and you need at least 3 or four to be satisfied. No, tacos are not really that cheap, defiantly as they can or should be. When eating out, getting a nice fat Burrito filled with rice & beans, cheese and the meat of your choice; Chicken, Beef, or Pork is much more filling. Usually a burrito is gong to cost you about $8.50 more or less, not too bad. But if you have kids the money starts piling up, so why not make them at home?

Usually when I make a big batch of Chili it's mostly for the purpose of making Tacos and Burritos for the next 5 days or so. Once the Chili is made, all I have to do to *make a nice fat tasty Burrito* for myself and whoever else is around. I *heat up the Chili and Beans, heat the tortilla, and assemble my Burrito by filling it with the Chili, Beans, Cheese, Cilantro, and Tomato and Scallions or whatever else I want*, and I've got myself a *Badass tasty dam Burrito in no time flat.* Now what's better than that I ask you? Not much.

Let me give you a little scenario on the economics of making your own tacos or burritos or whatever. It will cost me roughly $1.50 to make one of these Burritos, which is $6.00 for the four of them. At the cheapest if you buy 4 Burritos to take out and they're $8.50 a piece which is the average price of a burrito these days, those 4 burritos are going to cost you $34.00 on the low end. As we've already stated making the 4 Burritos at home is going to cost you $6.00 … You don't have to be a genius to figure out that you've just save yourself $28 … Dam! That's quite substantial. If you multiply that by lets say 30 times that you might make these burritos at home for the family, that would be about $1,020 for 30 trips to a restaurant for burritos or tacos in a year. Making burritos or tacos 30 times in a year at home is going to cost you about $180 … Subtract the $180 it cost to make you the Burritos at home from the $1,020 cost of getting Burritos to take out for the family 30 times in a year and you get $840 that you saved for the year by making the Burritos (or tacos) at home. That's some serious cash, wouldn't you say? If you have a bigger family, you will save even more, over $1,000 or more. Money you can put in the bank, put towards a vacation, buy Christmas presents with or whatever you please. The money is yours, and this is something to think about. Agreed?

MAKING THE BURRITO :

Heat your Chili (From one of the recipes in the book).

Cut up fresh, Tomatoes, Scallions, or Onions.

Get grated Cheddar, Monterey Jack or any cheese you like.

Heat your tortillas.

Fill the tortillas with Chili, Beans, Tomatoes, Scallions, Cilantro, Mexican Rice (next recipe), Avocado and whatever you like.

NOTE: To make tacos which are smaller, you use smaller tortillas and just fold them in-half and not into a package as you do for a Burrito. And you will generally serve 3-4 tacos to on fat Burrito.

INGREDIENTS For Your BURRITOS & / or TACOS :

Grilled or Boil Chicken, Chili, Pulled Pork, Cheese, fresh chopped Tomatoes, Beans, Cilantro, Avocado, Sour Cream, Scallions, Peppers.

To make Tacos or Burritos you just pick your Meat or Fish, and whatever of the above ingredients you like. It's as simple as that!

MEXICAN RICE

Here's some nice tasty Mexican Rice that's perfect for stuffing into your Burritos or serving as a side dish for any kind of meat, chicken, or fish.

INGREDIENTS :

1 cup Long Grain Rice
2 cups Chicken Broth, ¼ cup water
6 tablespoons Olive Oil
3 cloves Garlic, peeled and chopped fine
1 small Onion, peeled and chopped fine
3 tablespoons Tomato Paste
¼ teaspoon Kosher Salt
½ teaspoon ground Cumin, 1 Bay Leaf

Place the Olive Oil and onions in a medium sized pot and cook on low heat for 5 minutes. Add the Garlic and cook on low heat for 2 minutes. Add the Tomato Paste and cook on medium heat for two minutes.

Add the Rice, salt, Chicken Broth, and water and bring to the boil. Once all comes to the boil, lower heat to the lowest possible flame, cover the pot leaving the lid slightly askew and let the rice cook until done and all the liquid has evaporated, about 20-22 minutes.

Remove from heat, and uncover. Let stand for 7 minutes. Add the Black Pepper and Cumin and mix thoroughly into the rice. It's ready to serve.

OLD FASHIONED MEATLOAF

Nothing beats a good old meatloaf, and that's exactly what we've got here, a good old fashion American Meatloaf, great for dinner one night and sandwiches the next day.

INGREDIENTS :

8-ounces of Button Mushrooms, washed roughly chop & sauté for 6 minute with the onions a & garlic …
1 medium Onion, peeled and diced fine
2 cloves Garlic, peeled and minced fine
1 ½ pounds fresh Ground Beef
1 Egg
½ cup Seasoned Bread Crumbs
¼ teaspoon Salt & ½ teaspoon Black Pepper
6 Tablespoons Tomato Ketchup
3 Tablespoons chopped Fresh Parsley (Optional)

GLAZE :

8 tablespoons Ketchup, 1 /12 Brown Sugar
1 tablespoon Dijon Mustard

After you cook the Mushrooms & onions, set aside and let cool completely, about 15 minutes.

Place all the remaining ingredients, not including ingredients for the glaze into a large mixing bowl. Mix all the ingredients thoroughly with your hands.

Pre-Heat your oven to 350 degrees.

Grease a Loaf Pan with vegetable oil or butter. Place ground beef mixture in loaf-pan and press meat down, then bang the loaf pan a couple times to prevent air spaces.

Mix the 8 tbs. Ketchup, Mustard and Brown Sugar together and brush over the top of the meatloaf.

Place the meatloaf in the oven and bake at 350 degrees for about 1 hour and 15 minutes.

After about 1 ¼ hours, remove Meatloaf from oven and let cool on counter for about 15 minutes. Remove from pan.

Cut Meatloaf into 1 ½ to 2" slices and serve with potato, vegetable or salad.

BLUE RIBBON MEATLOAF

INGREDIENTS :

1 ½ pounds ground Beef
¾ cup Quaker Oats or Irish Oatmeal
1 egg
1 small Onion, peeled and chopped fine
½ teaspoon kosher or Sea Salt
½ teaspoon ground Black Pepper
½ cup Tomato Ketchup

GLAZE :

½ cup Heinz Chili Sauce

Pre-Heat oven to 350 degrees.

Place first 7 ingredients in a large mixing bowl and mix completely with your hands.

Grease a 8 X 4 inch baking pan with butter. Press the meatloaf into the pan.

Top the meatloaf with the Chili Sauce.

Bake in a 350 degree oven for 1 hour.

Remove the meatloaf from the oven and let rest for 15 minutes before serving.

MAKING THE PERFECT BURGER

Forget all the fancy different types of Burgers out there these days. Nothing beats a Classic No-Fuss straightforward Burger. It's all about the Burger, the meat and cooking it just right. Classic garnishes are the best; Ketchup, Cheese, maybe Mustard, a slice of Pickle, Onions raw or fried. If you want, you can put on a slice of Tomato and some Lettuce, but true purists like myself feel like once you start putting on that much stuff it starts taking away from the Burger flavor, you tasting the tomato and lettuce and less of the Beef Flavor which of course is the Star of this game here. No, all you really need is; Salt, Pepper, Cheese, 2 thin slices of Pickle and a little bit of onion is OK and your all set to go, a Classic Cheeseburger, there aren't many things better.

RECIPE :

1 ¼ lb. Ground Beef (15-20% fat)
Salt & Pepper
4 or 8 slices good quality American or Cheddar Cheese
4 Hamburger Buns
2 tablespoons vegetable oil
Ketchup (Heinz is the Best)

OPTIONAL INGREDIENTS :

Sliced raw Onion or sautéed Onions, Bacon, Mustard, Pickles, Lettuce, Tomato

Divide the Ground Beef into 4 equal parts. Shape Beef into Patties about ½ inch thick.

Heat a frying pan (Skillet) over medium heat for 3 minutes. Add oil, and heat 15 seconds. Turn flame up to high. Add raw beef patties. Cook 2 minutes. Season burgers with Salt & Pepper. Turn heat down to medium, cook for two minutes..

Turn heat back up to high. Turn burgers over to other side. Cook for 3 minutes until Burgers are about medium well, which is the Best way to cook a burger. Cook a little less if you want a medium Burger and less still if you want your cooked Burger Medium Rare.

BURGER NOTES: To cook your Burgers on the back-yard grill, it usually takes about 6 minutes to cook a Half-Inch Thick Burger depending on the heat of the grill, about 4 minutes on the first side and then you turn the burger over and cook it two three minutes on the second side.

Also, make sure not to make the common era of flipping your burger several time. You need to flip it once to get the best results. Yes, just once. That's it, 1 Tim, and as Roberto Duran would say, "No Mas!"

A good trick for you to know, which most home cooks do not know is that you can use a knife to poke into the center of the burger to see how much it is cooked in the center. If you look into the center and see it is rare than you would like it to be cooked, then you will know that you have a few more minutes to cook it.

This is a great trick to know for all cooking, so get in the habit of doing it as it is one of the greatest pieces of cooking knowledge you'll ever get. This is particularly good method to use when cooking chicken or turkey to look inside to see if the bird is cooked through or if it is still a little raw and you'll need to cook it more.

As we have laid out instructions to cook a Burger on an outdoor grill as many like to cook them this way. We will reiterate that personally, we feel cooking a Burger cooked in a pan or a Flat-Top-Grill where the Burger can cook in its own fat is the Best way. It gives the burger more flavor, and the burger gets evenly browned, but if you want to cook the burgers on an outdoor grill, that's your choice and your prerogative as the Stranger would say.

COPYCAT SHAKE SHACK
Burger & Sauce

Who doesn't love a Shake Shack Burger? Well some I guess, but not many. But they're dam hard to get. Forget about the money, that's nothing. Who has time to waste on those dam line? A lot would be the answer to that question, but not me. Yes I love those Burgers, but I don't do lines, so when I get a hankering for one, here's what I do. I simply make my own Shack Burgers, and you can too! The recipe is below and it's awesome! Want a Shack Burger but don't have the time to wait on line? Here you go.

The SAUCE :

¾ cup Mayonnaise
2 tablespoons Ketchup
2 tablespoons Yellow Mustard
½ teaspoon Garlic Powder, ½ teaspoon Paprika

Place all above ingredients in a bowl and mix together.

REMAINING INGREDIENTS :

8 ounces ground Beef Sirloin
8 ounces ground Beef Chuck
4 tablespoons Canola Oil
1 ½ tablespoons Butter
4 Martins Potato Rolls (Hamburger Rolls)
Kosher Salt & Black Pepper
4 slices Green Leaf Lettuce (or Boston Bibb)

8 slices of a ripe Plum Tomato, 8 slices of Dill Pickle
Break the rolls in-half and toast with butter in a skillet.

Place the ground sirloin and ground beef chuck in a bowl and gently mix together. After you mix the meat together, divide into four equal pieces and form into Burger Patties. Season both sides of the patties with Salt & Black Pepper.

Put oil in a medium sized heavy bottom skillet and turn heat on to medium-high flame. Add the Burger Patties to the pan and cook for 2 ½ minutes. Press burgers down just once to flatten slightly.

Turn burgers over and cook for 2 ½ minutes. Press down just once. The burgers are done.

Place the four bottoms of the rolls on 4 separate plates. Top with 2 slices of Pickles each. Place one cooked Burger on top of the pickles. Top the Burger with a little Shack Sauce, then place one lettuce leaf on top of this. Place two Tomato Slices that have been season with a little salt & pepper on top of the lettuce. Top with the top of the bun and serve.

BADASS LOBSTER ROLLS

There's nothing quite like a New England Lobster Roll, which are always an extra special Luxurious Treat to eat. They're one of my All-Time Favorites and I always feel great when I get a chance to eat one, and you should too. Make them and treat yourself and family or friends, you deserve it and anyone you make them for will be eternally grateful. I guarantee!

INGREDIENTS :

2 – 1 ¼ pound Lobsters
1 small baking Potato, peeled and cut to ½ inch dice
2 Celery Stalks, washed and sliced thin
2 tablespoons chopped Chives
5 tablespoons Mayonnaise
Kosher Salt
Ground Black Pepper
6 Hot Dog Rolls
2 tablespoons soft Butter

Cook the potatoes in a small pot of boiling salted water fro 3 minutes at a rapid boil. Remove from pot and strain in a colander. Set aside to cool.

Cook the Lobsters in a large pot of boiling water for 8 - 10 minutes ant the boil. Remove lobsters from the pot and let cool in a large pan.

After the lobsters have cooled down, beak the shells and remove all the lobster meat from the tail, claws and knuckles.

Cut the Lobster Meat into ¾" pieces and place in a glass bowl. Season the Lobster Meat with a pinch of Salt and a generous amount of ground Black Pepper and mix. Add the mayonnaise and mix. Add the Chives and mix.

Gently open the Hot Dog Rolls being careful not to break the rolls in half. Spread butter on the insides of

the rolls and place in a 350 degrees oven until the rolls start getting slightly browned, about 4 to 5 minutes. Remove from oven and let cool for 3 minutes. Stuff all the Hot Dog Rolls equally with the dressed Lobster Meat, serve and enjoy, these Puppy's are an extra special treat.

McRIB

The McRib, you either *love it,* or hate. Well I love them and like my fellow McRib Lovers I've often felt deprived when it's not around, which is most of the time. Which you probably know, the McRib is a sandwich made with ground pork that mimics a rack of pork ribs. It's topped with pickles, onions, and of course lots of yummy Barbecue Sauce on a toasted roll. Oh, and yes, the McRib was created and is sold by McDonalds. It was first invented in 1981 and is offered periodically as a limited-time-only item that is never on the permanent menu. This last fact is much to the chagrin of those of us who love it just can't get enough of it. You know what I'm talking about, the McRib has gone years without ever being offered at McDonalds anywhere. That's how it is with the McRib.

So, if you love these tasty little morsels of a sandwich and just can't take it, only being able to eat your favorite sandwich just a few times every few years or so with no McRibs in-between, you unfair ordeal is over. Now with this recipe below, you can now indulge in a tasty McRib and time at all. You've got a McRib craving, just go to the supermarket, get the ingredients, make them, and indulge.

COPYCAT RECIPE :

INGREDIENTS:

2 ¼ pounds Ground Pork Shoulder
1 tablespoons Sugar
1 ½ teaspoons Kosher Salt
1 teaspoon ground Black Pepper

Place above ingredients in a large bowl and mix together. Once mixed, divide the ground pork mixture into 6 equal sized portions.
Shape each portion of meat into a rectangle 6 ½ X 3 ½ inches each. Take a chopstick or handle of a table knife and make 5 crosswise impressions into the patty that will mimic the look of a slab of Pork Spare Ribs.

Place the six formed patties onto a small sheet-pan or cookie pan and place in the freezer for 1 hour.

REMAINING INGREDIENTS & PREPARATION :

4 tablespoons Canola Oil (or other vegetable oil)
1 small Onion, peeled and chopped
2 Dill Pickles, sliced
1 /12 cups of your favorite Barbecue Sauce (Heinz, Hunts, etc.)
6 – 6" Hero Rolls

Place oil in a medium sized skillet and cook three of the patties over medium heat until the patties are golden brown and cooked through (cook 4 minutes on each side).

When all the patties are cooked, place back on the cookie pan and coat each side of Pork Patties with Barbecue Sauce. Cook in a 350 degree oven for 5-6 minutes.

While the Pork Patties (McRibs) are cooking, toast the insides of all the Hero Rolls in the same skillet that the Pork Patties cooked in.

Remove Pork Patties from the oven. To assemble, place a bottom part of Hero Roll down on a place. Top the roll with a Pork Patty. Place 3 slices of pickle over each patty, and sprinkle on some chopped Onion over the patty. Top with a Hero Roll top. Repeat this process until you have 6 McRib Sandwiches. Enjoy!

BADASS SLOPPY JOES

Sloppy Joe's have been an American favorite for almost 100 years now. There popularity is due in part to their tastiness and that American's sure love beef, but even more so is the affordability and quick and easy cooking preparation. Kids especially love them and they are really geared to kids more-so than adults. This being said, there is no age limit on these tasty little sandwiches that are for not just young children but kids of all ages, so if you haven't had them in a while, why not give them a go and relive part of your childhood while you're at it. Enjoy!

INGREDIENTS :

1 medium Bell Pepper, seed and chopped fine
1 medium Onion, peeled and chopped fine
4 Garlic cloves, peeled and minced
1 pound Ground Beef
½ teaspoon Kosher Salt
½ teaspoon ground Black Pepper
½ teaspoon Sweet Paprika
1 – 15 ounce can Tomato Puree
½ cup Ketchup
1 tablespoon Worcestershire Sauce
3 tablespoons Brown Mustard
4 -6 Hamburger Buns

Place the Canola Oil and Green Peppers in a large skillet pan and turn heat on to low. Cook Peppers on low flame for 8 minutes. Add onions and cook on medium heat for 6 minutes.

Add the Garlic and cook on low heat for 2 minutes.

Add the beef and cook on medium heat until the beef loses its raw color, about 5 minutes. Add the Salt, Black Pepper, and Paprika and cook on low heat for 3 minutes.

Add the Worcestershire Sauce, Ketchup, and Tomato Puree and cook over low heat for 15 minutes. Add the Mustard, cook one minute on low heat. Turn heat off.

Toast Hamburger Buns, divide the Sloppy Joe Sauce evenly amongst the buns and serve.

BARBECUED PORK SANDWICHES

These sandwiches are friggin awesome. All but staunch vegetarians will absolutely love them. Make these sandwiches, cook up some Corn on The Cob, Potato Salad, get your beverages, and get yourself a nice big Watermelon and you can have an awesome Southern Style Picnic or backyard party with very little effort at all.

DRY RUB :

1 ½ tablespoons Kosher Salt
1 ½ tablespoons Ground Black Pepper
2 tablespoons Smoked Paprika
2 ½ tablespoons Brown Sugar
½ teaspoon Cayenne Pepper
½ teaspoon each of Cumin and Cinnamon

1- 4 & 1/2 pound Pork Shoulder (Pork Butt)
2 large Onions, peeled and roughly chopped
1/8 cup Olive Oil

Mix all above dry ingredients together in a bowl. Rub the dry rub all over the Pork Shoulder.

Place the onions on the bottom of a roasting pan. Drizzle olive oil over onions and mix. Place Pork Shoulder on top of the onions.

Cover the pan with aluminum foil and roast in a 325 degree oven until you can pull away the meat from the bone with a for, about 4 to 4 ½ hours. Remove from the oven. Remove aluminum foil and let rest for 15 minutes.

Shred the pork off the bone and place in a large mixing bowl. Pour in the cooking liquid and mix. Add 1 /12 cups Bad Ass Barbecue Sauce, or any BBQ Sauce you like and mix. Do not over-sauce. To serve, place some Barbecued Pork on top of a Potato Roll or Hamburger Bun and top with a little bit of Cole Slaw. Serve Sandwiches to everyone and Enjoy! You know you will!

COLE SLAW

1 small head of Green Cabbage, outer leaves removed
2 tablespoons Cider Vinegar (or White Vinegar)
1 teaspoon Kosher Salt, ½ teaspoon Black Pepper
1 teaspoon Paprika
2 tablespoons Brown or Dijon Mustard
2 tablespoons Olive Oil
¾ to 1 cup of Mayonnaise

Slice the Cabbage into thin slivers and place in a large mixing bowl. Add vinegar and salt and mix. Let set for 15 minutes, mixing two or three times as the cabbage marinates.

Place the cabbage in a colander and let the liquid drain off. Add Paprika, Black Pepper and Olive Oil and mix. Add mustard and mix. Add Mayonnaise and Mix.

CHICK-a FILET SANDWICHES

INGREDIENTS :

2 Boneless Chicken Breasts
1/3 cup Pickle Juice
1/3 cup Milk
2 Eggs
¾ cup Flour
1 tablespoon Powdered Sugar
½ teaspoon Paprika
½ teaspoon Salt
½ teaspoon Black Pepper
¼ teaspoon Garlic Powder

1 cup Canola or Peanut Oil for frying
2 Hamburger Buns
1 tablespoon Butter
8 slices Dill Pickle

Place the 2 Chicken Breasts between 2 sheets of Plastic Wrap. Pound the chicken breasts with a meat mallet until they are about ¾" thick. Cut each breast in-half and place in a bowl with the Pickle Juice and Marinate for 30 minutes.

Get a large mixing bowl, add flour to the bowl. Add, Salt, Black Pepper, Paprika, Sugar, and Garlic Powder to the flour and mix.

Heat the oil in a large skillet to 350 degrees for frying. Add Milk & Eggs to another bowl and beat together. Dip each of the 4 pieces of chicken into the eggs.

Shake off excess eggs from chicken and each into the flour mixture from the chicken and place into the hot oil and fry. Fry the Chicken 2 minutes on each side until each side is golden brown and cooked through. Place the cooked chicken on paper towels to soak up excess oil.

Split Hamburger Buns in-half and toast in a pan with the butter.

Set down 4 bottom halves of the Hamburger Buns. Place two Pickle Slices on top of the Buns. Add a piece of Fried Chicken on top, place top part of each bun on top of the Chicken and serve.

NOTE : Add a little Mayonnaise if you like, or for something *Extra Special*, top the Chicken with a little Cole Slaw (Recipe Above) and serve the *Tastiest Chicken Sandwiches Ever!*

EGG SALAD SANDWICHES

Egg Salad Sandwiches? They don't get a whole lot of attention when it comes to American food-stuff or any kind of food for that matter. It's like they are there, they do their job and no one pays any attention to them. Yes they do there job, and their job is to be a very tasty sandwich that's quick and easy to make, cost very little yet satisfies a whole lot. What more could you as of any type of food? Not much I tell you! Yet the sandwich gets no respect. No matter, maybe that's just the way it's supposed to be, it's a wonderful thing, that doesn't get much fanfare, yet millions are eaten every year by many Americans who seem to love it, and that's just the way it gotta be. The Egg Salad Sandwich, hugely popular without much respect. C'est la Vie.

INGREDIENTS :

6 Extra Large Eggs
1 cup Mayonnaise
2 tablespoons Dijon Mustard (optional)
½ teaspoon ground Black Pepper and a pinch of Salt

Place Eggs in a pot with enough water to cover pass the eggs by a half inch or so. Bring the water to the boil. Lower water to a gentle simmer and let the eggs cook for 8 minutes.

Turn flame off and drain the hot water from the pan. Leave the eggs in the pot and run cold water over the eggs for two minutes. Drain off water and let eggs cool in the refrigerator for about 45 minutes.

Peel shells off the cooled boiled eggs. Slice eggs in-half and put the yolks in a mixing bowl and the white on a cutting board.

Mash the yolks with a fork. Add the mustard, salt, pepper, and half of the mayonnaise to the bowl and mix.

Chop the egg whites on a cutting board into a 1/8th inch dice.

Add the chopped egg whites and the remainder of the mayonnaise to the mixing bowl with egg yolk mixture and mix together.

The Egg Salad is done and ready to be made into sandwiches or to be one component of a cold composed Salad Plate.

THE BOMBER

Here's a Breakfast Sandwich that's really Badass. It's called the Bomber. It's made with all sorts of things that a Badass might like, or anyone who has quite the hearty appetite. It's a Breakfast Sandwich made with Home Fries, Bacon, Taylor Ham, and Eggs, and it's a doozy, I'm sure you'll agree. It's made for breakfast, but it's great any time of the day.

INGREDIENTS :

2 Eggs
2 slices of Taylor Ham
2 slices of Bacon
Home Fries, from recipe in the book
1 Kaiser Roll, or Hero Roll

Place the eggs in a small bowl and add a pinch each of Salt & Black Pepper and beat.

Cook the Taylor Ham in a skillet with a couple tablespoons of oil. Cook over medium heat until the Taylor Ham is lightly browned on both sides, about 4 minutes.

Remove the Taylor Ham from pan and set aside. Add the Bacon to the pan and cook on medium heat to the degree of doneness you like your Bacon. I myself don't like it as hard and crispy as others, so you cook it according to the way you like it.

Remove the bacon from the pan and set aside with the Ham. Drain off most of the grease from the pan, leaving enough behind to cook the eggs in. Cook the eggs scrambling them until full cooked.

Split the roll in-half and add a few slices of Home Fries to the bottom half of the roll. Top the Home Fries with the eggs, then add the Taylor Ham and top with the Bacon. Top the sandwich with the top half of the roll, serve and enjoy.

CHICKEN SALAD

INGREDIENTS:

1 small Chicken, ¾ cup Real Mayonnaise
½ teaspoon Salt
2 tablespoons Olive Oil, 1 Bay Leaf
1 tablespoon Dijon or Brown Mustard
½ teaspoon ground Black Pepper
2 stalks of Celery, washed and cut to ¼" pieces

Place the Chicken Bay Leaf and half the Salt in a pot and fill with water to cover the chicken. Turn heat on to high and bring the water to the bowl. Once the water starts boiling, lower the heat so the water is at a medium simmer. Let the chicken simmer for 45 minutes, then turn the heat off. Let the chicken set in the pot with the heat off for 20 minutes.

Remove the chicken from the pot set in a colander and let cool for 20 minutes. Remove all the Chicken meat from the bone and place in a large bowl. Break or dice the chicken into ¾" pieces. Add the salt, Black Pepper, & Olive Oil and mix with the Chicken. Add the Mustard, Mayonnaise, and Celery and mix.

You now have Chicken Salad and it's dam tasty. Place it between a couple slices of bread, top with some lettuce and you're good to go. If you don't want to put it on a sandwich just eat the Chicken Salad on a plate over some lettuce and maybe a couple wedges of tomato on the side. Enjoy.

HOW to COOK The PERFECT STEAK

Who doesn't love a good Steak? Not man I tell you. For many, especially American men Steak is the ultimate culinary treat. Yes American males love it, and it's a symbol of our great country. But how many know how to make a great steak? Some, but not many in the scheme of things. Well if you do want to cook your own steak and cook it properly, the direction are below.

INGREDIENTS :

1 "PRIME" SIRLOIN STEAK 10 to 14 ounces
Ground Black Pepper and Kosher or Sea Salt
Butter
Vegetable Oil

Season your Steak with Salt and Pepper on both Sides.

Heat a frying pan over high heat for 3 minutes.

Put 2 tablespoons of oil in pan. Heat oil for 10 seconds, then add steak to pan. Medium Rare is the best temperature for a steak.

It's going to depend how thick your steak is for its cooking time. A good trick in cooking your steak is periodically peaking inside the steak by making a slit with a sharp thin knife and looking in the middle of the steak.

Cook your steak over high heat for three minutes, lower the heat to medium and cook two minutes more. Raise the heat to high and flip your Steak over to the other side.

Cook the steak for two minutes, then cut and look inside to the middle of the steak to see if you want to take the steak off the fire, or if you want to cook it for 2, 3, or 4 minutes more depending on if you want your steak Medium Rare, Medium, or Well Done.

When the Steak is done. Put it on a plate with whatever type potato or vegetable you'd like. Take a half-teaspoon of butter and spread it over your Steak and add a little more Salt and Pepper if you'd like. Enjoy!

LONDON BROIL

London Broil was once an All-American Classic that was all the rage way back in the 50's, 1960s and 70's .. My mother cooked it all the time. We never had Sirloin, it was too expensive.

So "why," you say was London Broil so popular back then? Why? Well, it's cheap and fairly tasty. We say fairly tasty, as it can be quite good, but definitely not as good as a juicy Sirloin or Rib Eye Steak, which have much higher fat contents making for juicier, more tender cuts of meat. However, they are much more *expensive,* double to triple the price per pound of the much cheaper Flank Steak known all over America as London Broil.

London Broil's popularity is attributed to the fact that multitudes of Americans Love their Steak, and for those on a budget, maybe the Flank Steak affords them the opportunity to eat steak when they might otherwise not be able to afford one of those New York Cut Sirloin Steaks. London Broil aka the Flank Steak affords them an opportunity to get their "Steak Fix" at a reasonable price.

Two things to know if you're going to cook a London Broil. Number One, it has to be cooked at about Medium Rare. If cooked longer, it gets quite tough. At Medium Rare it stays somewhat tender. So if you don't eat Medium Rare meat and like yours cooked Med Well or Well Done, "Forget about having London Broil," it's not for you. Number two, though Flank Steak isn't the tastiest cut in the land, you can fix it up to make it taste even better. Some nice Mushrooms sautéed in butter or a quick pan sauce work wonders.

London Broil can be cooked on a Backyard Grill or as I prefer in a Skillet in your kitchen. One very important point is that I don't recommend cooking it under a Household Broiler. This is the "WORST THING" you could ever do when cooking London Broil or some other cut of meat, do not use the Broiler, it doesn't get hot enough and using a heavy bottom frying pan will net you superior results, "Trust me."

COOKING LONDON BROIL

1 fresh Flank Steak
Kosher or Sea Salt and Ground Black Pepper
2 tablespoons Sweet or Lightly Salted Butter
2 tablespoons vegetable oil (Corn, Canola, Soy)
6 tablespoons of Red or White Wine or water
2 teaspoons Gravy Master or Maggi's

Season the Flank Steak with salt & pepper.

Heat your Skillet over a high flame for two minutes. Add 2 Tablespoons vegetable oil to pan.

Add the Flank Steak and cook for 3 minutes. Turn the steak over and cook for another 3 minutes over high heat.

Turn the flame down to medium and cook Steak for 2 minutes more on each side. Take steak out of pan and put on a platter to rest for a few minutes.

Put wine or water in pan that you cooked the Steak in. Scrape bottom of pan to dislodge the brown bits sticking to pan, there is an abundance of flavor in these brown bits which will Help Make your delicious sauce). Add Gravy Master.

Let liquid reduce to half its original volume.

Turn flame off. Add butter to pan and move Pan in a circular motion so the butter will mix in with pan juices, making your tasty sauce.

Quickly slice your Flank Steak across the grain which is cutting across the shorter end of the Steak. Slice to about 1/8 of an inch thick.

Place meat on everyone's plate with potato and or vegetable of your choice. Spoon sauce of London Broil and Enjoy!

NOTE: You do not have to make the sauce if you think it might be too difficult. If so, you can stop after step 5 and continue to step 10 and the slicing and serving of the London Broil. You can also use your favorite bottled Steak Sauce if you choose to.

Another way the Dude likes to serve his London Broil or any Steak is with sauté some sautéed mushrooms. Sauté them in butter with salt & pepper and serve over the London Broil.

And along with the London Broil or any Steak, Dude usually serves his Dads Home-Fries and if in season 2 or 3 slices of nice Beefsteak Tomato's sprinkled with salt.

Serve with; Baked, Boiled, or Mashed Potatoes, and some Green Veg or Buttered Carrots. Whatever? Just enjoy!

CHICKEN FRANCESE

Chicken Francese, now isn't that *Fancy?* Chicken Francese used to be a popular dish back in the 1960's & 70's .. Chicken Francese is a hugely popular dish in Rochester New York, so much so that some have suggested the dish be called Chicken Rochester. As of this date, that has not happened. It is said that Italian Immigrants to Rochester brought their recipes with them, including Veal Francese and substituted chicken for the more expensive Veal in Veal Francese. The rest is history.

INGREDIENTS :

4 skinless boneless Chicken Breast
1 cup Flour
½ teaspoon each of Salt & Black Pepper
3 Eggs
¼ cup Canola Oil (or any Vegetable Oil)
½ stick Butter
1/3 cup Dry White Wine
¼ cup water
¼ cup fresh chopped Parsley
2 Lemons, juice one and cut the other into thin slices

Place the chicken breast between 2 pieces of plastic wrap and pound with a meat mallet until all the breast are ¼" thick.

Season both sides of each chicken breast with salt & pepper.

Place the flour in one shallow bowl with ½ teaspoon each of salt & pepper and mix.

Place the eggs in another shallow bowl, season with salt & pepper and beat the eggs. Place the oil in a large skillet and heat to high.

Dredge each piece of chicken in the flour, shake off excess four and then dip in to the eggs and coat completely. Shake off excess egg and put immediately into the pan with the hot oil. Do this with all four pieces of chicken.

Cook the chicken for two minutes on each side, then remove from pan and place on paper towels and keep warm.

Drain off all the oil from the pan.

Add the water, wine, and Lemon Juice to pan and cook on high heat until the liquid is reduced by half, about 5 minutes.

Turn the heat of and add the butter and chopped Parsley to the pan and swirl the pan in a circular direction to emulsify the sauce.

Place the Chicken Breast onto four plates. Pour the sauce over each chicken breast, and top the chicken with Lemon slices and serve.

CLASSIC BEEF STEW

Beef Stew, it's long been an American favorite. Beef Stew is a full & hearty dish that will warm the cockles of your Heart on a cold Winters day. With all the vegetables in this stew; Carrots, Mushrooms, and Potatoes, you don't need a whole lot of meat, unless you really want it. With the carrots and potatoes, 5-6 ounces of meat per person is plenty. And if you serve the stew as I like to do, which is over a bed of Egg Noodles, your stew will stretch even further. If you've never had the stew over noodles, try it some time, it's sure to please. So, I do hope you make this stew, add it to your repertoire, and enjoy.

RECIPE :

3 pound Beef Chuck, cut into 2" cubes
¼ cup Olive Oil
1 medium Onion, peeled and diced
10 ounces Button Mushrooms, sliced thick
½ cup dry Red Wine
4 Garlic cloves, peeled and sliced
4 Carrots, peeled and cut into large dice
1 cup crushed Tomatoes
2 tablespoons Tomato Paste
1 Beef Bullion Cube (optional), 2 Bay Leaves
2 Baking Potatoes, peeled an cut in large dice
2 sprigs fresh Rosemary
½ teaspoon each Sea Salt & Black Pepper
½ lb. package wide Egg Noodles, ¼ cup chopped fresh Parsley

Place half the olive oil in a 6-quart pot and cook mushrooms over medium until lightly browned. Add onions and cook for 4 minutes on low heat. Add ¼ teaspoon each of slat & black pepper and cook 1 minute more. Remove from pot and set aside.

Place remaining olive oil in the pot and turn heat on to high. Brown the beef in 3 separate batches over medium to high heat until all the beef is nicely browned.

Set the beef aside when all the pieces are browned. Add 3 tablespoons of flour to pan and cook on low heat in the oil and pan drippings from the beef, while stirring with a wooden spoon. Cook 4-5 minutes.

Add wine and turn heat on to high and let cook until the wine reduces by half, about 4-5 minutes.

Add 1 ½ cups of water a little at a time while stirring to mix flour and water together, cooking over a medium flame for 3 minutes.

Add beef back top pot and sprinkle the beef with a little salt and pepper.

Add tomatoes, tomato paste, carrots, garlic, and bay leaf. Put the mushrooms & onions back in the pot and cook on high heat for 5 minutes.

Add water to just barely cover the meat. Add bullion cube. Bring to the boil. Once all comes to the boil, lower to a steady simmer and let cook for 1 hour and ten minutes.

Add potatoes to pot and continue cooking until the beef is nice and tender, about 25 minutes more. Turn heat off.

Cook the egg noodles according to directions on package. When done cooking drain in a colander. Put the noodles back in the pot they cooked in and add the butter. Mix.

Place some noodles on each plate for your guest, then top with a good portion of the stew for each plate. Drizzle with a little olive oil and sprinkle a little chopped parsley on each plate and serve.

SHEPHERD'S PIE alla KEEF
Keith Richard's That Is !!!

Yes *Keef*, as in Keith Richards of *The Rolling Stones*, the World's Greatest Rock-N-Roll Band *ever!* But you know that. This is the way Keith likes his Shepherds Pie, as does The Dude, and you will too. If it's good enough for Keef, it's good enough for the Dude, and you too. Abide!

INGREDIENTS:

3 pounds Potatoes, peeled and diced
1 tablespoon Butter
Salt & Pepper to taste
2 large Onions, chopped
2 pounds Ground Beef
2 large Carrots, grated
2 – 12 oz. cans Beef Broth
5 tablespoons water
1 tablespoon Cornstarch

Put potatoes in a large pot of salted water. Bring the water to the boil. Lower to a simmer and cook the potatoes until tender, about 8 minutes.

Drain potatoes once cooked.

Put cooked, drained potatoes in a large mixing bowl with the butter and season with salt and black pepper. Mash potatoes with a potato - masher or whip with an electric mixer. If using a hand potato-masher, mash potatoes with masher, then mix with a wooden spoon until nicely whipped.

Heat a large frying-pan. Add 3 tablespoons of vegetable oil. Add ground-beef, cook over medium heat for 4 minutes. Add onions, continue cooking for minutes on high heat. Lower heat to low flame and cook 4 minutes more.

Add carrots and beef broth to pan. Mix cornstarch with water and add to pan. Cook over low flame for 8 minutes.

Add peas to pan, cook for 1 minute.

Pour Beef Mixture into a glass or ceramic baking dish. Evenly top beef with the mashed potatoes.

Bake in a 400-degree oven for 12 minutes, then place under the boiler until potatoes get nicely browned. Take care not to burn the potatoes once they are under the broiler.

Let cool slightly for 3 minutes and serve.

BRAISED LAMB SHANKS

Here's another nice hearty dish that's great for a cold winters day, or anytime at all. Serve the Lamb Shanks just as the recipe below says, or for something really nice, cook some Egg Noodles, butter them, and serve a Lamb Shank per person over the noodles and you'll be in Culinary Heaven. Enjoy!

RECIPE :

4 Lamb Shanks
4 Carrots, peeled
2 stalks Celery, washed and cut to small dice
2 medium Onion, peeled and chopped fine
6 cloves garlic, Peeled and chopped fine
¼ teaspoon each: Salt &Black Pepper
1 cup dry Red Wine
2 – 28 ounce can crushed Italian Tomatoes
5 tablespoons Tomato Paste
2 Idaho Potatoes, peeled and cut to large chunks
2 sprigs fresh Rosemary, 2 Bay Leafs
2 cups water
1 – 10 ounce box frozen Peas

Place olive oil in a 6-quart non-corrosive pot. Season lamb with salt & pepper. Place lamb in pot and brown over a medium-high flame until the lamb is browned on all sides, about 12 minutes.

Remove lamb from pot and set aside. Add celery to pot and cook on high heat until light brown, about 8 minutes.

Add onions and cook on medium heat for 5 minutes. Add garlic, lower heat and cook for 2 minutes.

Add the wine and cook on high heat until the wine is reduced by half of its original volume, about 7 minutes.

Add tomatoes, tomato paste, and water to the pot. Add the lamb back to the pot and bring the liquid to boil. As soon as the liquid starts boiling, lower the heat to low and let all simmer for 30 minutes.

Cut the peeled carrots into large chunks.

After the lamb has been cooking for 30 minutes add the Carrots to the pot. Cook 20 minutes more and add the potatoes, rosemary, and Bay Leafs to the pot.

Continue cooking on a low simmer until the lamb is tender, which should be about 25-35 minutes more for a total cooking time of about 1 hour and 20 minutes. Cook the peas in boiling salted water, then drain.

To serve, place one Lamb Shank along with some potatoes, carrots, and peas, and a bit of sauce, saving most of the sauce for pasta the next day.

OTHER STUFF ???

Other Stuff? Yeah whatever? Other Stuff, just what the name implies. Well maybe not. Hey this isn't your normal everyday run-of-the-mill cookbook. It's the Badass Cookbook and it's different, an awesome compilation of the dam tastiest most Badass recipes ever! That's a fact. So, Other Stuff, we got; Baked Beans, Mac N Cheese, Stuffed Cabbage, General Tso's Chicken, Spaghetti & Meatballs, Thanksgiving Turkey, Mashed Potatoes, Rutabagas, New England Clam Bake, and on-and-on. Lots of great stuff, *Other Stuff* in fact, the kind of Stuff you can't help but love. Try them out and go for them, you're sure to love what? Other Stuff! There's also San Francisco Fish Stew, Sweet Potatoes, French Toast, the Denver Omelet, Home Fries, and much more stuff. And don't pass up the recipe for Porchetta, Italy's answer to America's Barbecued Pork, or is it the other way around? Porchetta is one of the great roast meat dishes of the World, and if you've never had it, check it out and make it, it's in other stuff. And after other stuff, there's not a ton of desserts in the book, but there's some dam good ones, like; Bananas Foster, Oreo Cheesecake, & the *Best Chocolate Cookie Ever.* What more can anyone ask for? Well, this is the Badass Cookbook, and I hope you know by now it's the Best Most Badass collection of some of the World's Greatest Recipes Ever. The Badass Cookbook, you've got it, it'll give you years of joy and Happiness, so congratulations, you're one of the smart one's. You're a Badass! And we mean that only in the best of ways.

STUFFED CABBAGE

My mom used to make these Stuffed Cabbage at least once a month. Along with Meatloaf and Spaghetti & Meatballs, this was one of her best dishes, and we all loved them, and so will you.

INGREDIENTS :

1 medium onion, minced
3 cloves of garlic, minced
6 tablespoons chopped parsley
6 tablespoons bread crumbs
2 eggs, Salt & Pepper to taste
1 cup long grain rice, cooked
1 1/2 pounds Ground Beef
½ cup grated Pecorino Romano
1 medium Head Savoy Cabbage, about 2 lbs.
½ cup chicken broth
½ stick of Butter
¼ cup Olive Oil
2 cups tomato sauce

Cook rice according to directions on package, then let cool. You will end up with 2 cups rice.

Bring a large pot of salted water to the boil. Cut the bottom off of the cabbage. Cut the core out of the cabbage. Cook the cabbage in boiling water for 4-5 minutes, until the cabbage leaves are tender, yet still slightly firm. Drain cabbage and let cool.

In a large mixing bowl, add cooled the rice, onion, garlic, parsley, ground beef, and breadcrumbs.

Season the beef liberally with salt and pepper. Mix with hands.

Add cheese, a ½ cup of the tomato sauce, and eggs, and mix thoroughly.

Take a small handful of the meat mixture and fill each cabbage leave. Place a small amount of the meat mixture about 3 inches from the end of a cabbage leave. Fold the end over the meat. Fold sides in, and then roll cabbage leave up to close. Roll the cabbage leaves until all the meat mixture is gone.

Heat oven to 400 degrees. Coat a shallow glass or ceramic baking pan with the olive oil. Place half of the remaining tomato sauce into pan. Place all the rolled cabbages neatly into pan. Cover with remaining tomato sauce. Add chicken Broth and dot with butter on top.

Cook in oven at 400 degrees for 12 minutes. Lower heat to 350 and continue cooking for about 30 minutes until the meat inside the cabbage is fully cooked.

Take out of oven and let rest for 10 minutes before serving. Serve each person 3 or 4 Stuffed Cabbages with a little sauce. You may serve with roast, boiled, or mashed potatoes or whatever you like.

MAC & CHEESE

1 pound Elbow Macaroni
1 & ½ pound Cheddar Cheese, grated
3 tablespoons Butter
3 ½ tablespoons Flour, 3 ¼ cups Milk
½ teaspoon Salt & ½ teaspoon Black Pepper

Cook the Elbow Macaroni in boiling salted water according to the directions on the box. Drain in a colander, and sprinkle a couple tablespoons of Olive Oil over the macaroni and mix. Place the macaroni in a 9 X 13 glass baking dish.

Heat the Milk in a small pot until it comes to the boil, then turn heat off immediately.

Place 3-tablespoons Butter in another small pot and turn heat to low and melt the butter. Add the flour, turn heat to low and mix butter and flour with a wooden spoon. Cook until the mixture just starts to brown, then slowly start adding the milk as you whisk with a wire-whip. Slowly add all the milk. Cook until the sauce thickens, about 5 minutes on low heat while stirring. Remove from heat.

Add the salt & pepper and mix. Add the grated cheese and mix to the cheese until the cheese is completely melted. Pour the cheese sauce over the macaroni and mix thoroughly.

Bake in a 350 degree oven for 30 minutes. Remove from oven and let rest for 10 minutes before serving.

BADASS BAKED BEANS

Yes these Beans are Bad Ass, and people just love them. And yes Baked Beans are an all-time American favorite served at picnics, barbecues, and everyday meals at home. They're an essential side dish when eating Ribs, Barbecued Chicken and such. Serve them with Pork Chops, Fried Chicken or whatever and it's all good.

RECIPE :

1 pound bag dry Great Northern Beans (or Navy Beans)
1 pound of Smoke Bacon
1 large Onion, peeled and chopped
1 Green Bell Pepper, remove seeds & core, then chop the pepper
5 cloves Garlic, peeled and minced
1 cup of your favorite Barbecue Sauce
¼ cup Molasses
¼ cup Honey
½ cup Brown Sugar
2 oz. your favorite Bourbon (Jim Beam, Makers Mark)
2 tablespoons Smoked Paprika
3 tablespoon Mustard (Brown, Dijon, or Yellow)
3 tablespoons Apple Cider Vinegar
1 teaspoon Tabasco or your favorite Hot Sauce
1 teaspoon Kosher Salt
1 teaspoon Ground Black Pepper

Remove beans from bag and place in a bowl. Sift through the beans looking for pebbles or any foreign objects that are sometimes in the beans. Wash the beans. Place the washed beans in a large bowl and cover by 3 inches with water. Put in the refrigerator and let soak over night.

Remove the beans from the refrigerator, drain water off in a colander and wash the beans.

Cut all the Bacon into1 ½" long pieces. Place all the Bacon in a Dutch Oven or other large oven-proof pot. Cook on medium heat while stirring with a wooden spoon until the Bacon just starts to brown. Drain the Bacon in a colander to drain off fate, but reserve 5 tablespoon of the fat in the pan to cook the peppers & onions.

Set the bacon aside.

Place the Green Peppers and Onions in the pot and cook on low heat for 8 minutes while stirring with a wooden spoon. Add the garlic and cook on low heat for 3 minutes. Add Bourbon and cook on high heat for 3 minutes. Turn heat off. Remove the peppers & onions from pan and set aside with Bacon until later.

Place the dried soaked beans in the pot and fill with water to 2" above the beans. Cook on the stove-top until the beans are soft but still have a little bite to them, about 1 hour 15 minutes to 90 minutes.

Drain the beans, reserving the cooking liquid. Add beans back to pot and pour some of the cooking liquid just to bring up to the level of the beans. Add the Bacon, Peppers & Onions and all the remaining ingredients to the pot. Bring the liquid to the boil, then lower heat to a medium simmer. Let simmer on top of the stove for 15 minutes.

Place the pot or casserole in the oven and bake the beans at 350 degrees for 1 hour and 30 minutes. Remove from oven and let rest fro 12 minutes before serving.

BAD BETTY'S EASY BAKED BEANS

If you don't want to take the time or effort to make the above Bad Ass Baked Beans, these are a bit easier, take a lot less time to make and taste pretty dam good to boot. They're Bad Betty's famous recipe and they're sure to please and satisfy just about anyone. And PS, Betty's not really bad, it's just a nickname.

RECIPE :

1 pound Smoked Bacon, cut to 1" pieces
1 large Onion, peeled and chopped
1 Green Bell Pepper, seeded and chopped
6 cloves Garlic, peeled and minced
4 – 15 ounce cans Navy or Pinto Beans,
drained and washed
1 cup of your favorite BBQ Sauce (Badass or other)
¼ cup Molasses, ¼ cup Brown Sugar
3 tablespoons Brown or Dijon Mustard
1 teaspoon Kosher Salt, 1 teaspoon Black Pepper
1 ½ tablespoons Smoke Paprika

Place oil in a 3-quart pot and turn heat on to medium. Add Bacon and cook Bacon until it just starts getting browned, about 8-10 minutes. Remove the Bacon from pot and set aside.

Add the Green Peppers to pot and cook on low heat for 10 minutes while stirring. Add the onions and cook on medium heat for 6 minutes. Add garlic and cook on medium heat for 2 minutes.

Add all the remaining ingredients to the pot and cook on low heat while stirring occasionally for 20 minutes.

Place in a glass casserole dish and bake at 350 degrees for 20 minutes. Remove from the oven, let rest for 8 minutes, then serve.

Daniel Zwicke

PERFECT ROAST TURKEY

Turkey? It's the All-American dish that you can't do
Thanksgiving without. Have you ever cooked one? Do
you know how? Are you afraid? Don't worry many are.
Well one day may come when you've got to cook the
turkey. Don't fret! Here's the perfect way to roast one,
a Turkey that is. Just follow these easy steps, make
some tasty side dish and you good to go. Happy
Thanksgiving! And don't forget, it's not just for
Thanksgiving, but any time of the year

INGREDIENTS :

1 – 12-14 pound Turkey
1 ½ sticks Butter, softened
2 teaspoons Kosher Salt
1 teaspoon ground Black Pepper
2 tablespoons Flour
2 ¾ cups Chicken Broth
½ cup water

In a bowl mix the Salt & Black Pepper together with
the butter.

Preheat oven to 400 degrees. Wash the turkey, then pat
dry with clean paper towels.

Put a wire roasting rack in the large roasting pan that
you'll roast the turkey in. Rub the butter all over the
skin of the turkey.

Place the turkey in the oven and roast at 400 degrees for 30 minutes. Baste the turkey with the juices in the pan, getting the basting juices all over the turkey.

Turn the heat down to 325 degrees and cook the turkey until is cooked through. Baste the turkey every 20 to 30 minutes during this time. To check if the turkey is done, stick a meat thermometer into the thigh of the turkey. The thermometer should read 180 degrees and the turkey is done. If you don't have a meat thermometer, poke a turkey thigh with the tip of a sharp knife. If the liquid comes out clear, the turkey is done. If the liquid has blood in it, the turkey still needs to be a cook some more. In this case put the turkey back in the oven and check after 10 minutes.

One you have determined that the turkey is cooked through, remove from the oven and let rest for 15 minutes, while still in the pan, but out of the oven.

Remove the turkey from the pan and set on a carving board.

MAKING The GRAVY :

Heat the chicken broth in a small pot.

Pour off all of the fat from the pan, reserving ¼ cup of the fat in the pan. Place the roasting pan on top of the stove and turn flame on to low heat.

Add the flour to the pan and stir with a wooden spoon. Add a ½ cup of the hot chicken broth and cook while stirring with a whip. Add 1 more cup of the broth and continue cooking while stirring for 2 minutes more. Add remaining chicken broth and cook on low heat for 5 minutes as your stir. The Gravy is now ready. Strain the gravy through a wire sieve. Place gravy in a gravy boat and it's ready to go, to pour over your turkey and Mashed Potatoes.

MASHED POTATOES

Mashed Potatoes? If you had to pick America's All-Time favorite side dish, it would just have to be Mashed Potatoes! Is there anyone who doesn't love them, slathered with rich Butter, they're as soul satisfy and comforting as any food could ever wish to be. And when you think of Comfort Food, Mashed Potatoes no doubt heads the list, it's Pork Chops with Mashed Potatoes, Steak & Potatoes and what not. And as for Thanksgiving, it just not complete without the Turkey, Stuffing, and Mashed Potatoes, they're as American as Apple Pie.

5 large Russet, Maine, or Idaho Potatoes
1/3 cup of Whole Milk, hot.
3 tablespoons Butter, Salt & White Pepper

Place a 4-quart pot on stove and fill with water and 1 teaspoon salt. Peel potatoes and cut into for equal pieces. Add potatoes to water and bring back to the boil. Simmer for about 10 to 12 minutes or potatoes are just tender when pierced with a fork.

Remove potatoes from heat. Drain potatoes in a colander. Place potatoes back in the pot they cooked in, making sure all water has been drained and pot is dry.

Mash potatoes with hand potato masher. Add Butter and mix with a wooden spoon. Add Salt and Pepper to taste. Add the Hot Milk a little at a time, stirring w/ wooden spoon. Serve immediately.

SWEET POTATOES
Candied !!!

INGREDIENTS:

4 pounds Sweet Potatoes, washed
1 ½ sticks Butter
1 cup Brown Sugar
½ teaspoon Salt, ½ teaspoon Black Pepper

Place Sweet Potatoes in a pot and cover with water. Bring to the boil and cook until the Sweet Potatoes just start to get soft, about 14 minutes. Drain the potatoes in a colander and let them set and cool.

While the potatoes are cooking, place the Butter, Brown Sugar, Salt, and Pepper in a small sauce-pan and cook over low heat for 5 minutes as you stir with a wooden spoon.

Once the Sweet Potatoes have cooled, peel them then place in a 9" X 13" glass baking pan. Pour the butter / sugar mixture over the Sweet Potatoes and bake in a 350 degree oven for 15 minutes. Remove from oven and let the Sweet Potatoes cool slightly before serving with your Turkey or Chicken or whatever. Enjoy!

DANNY'S BADASS RUTABAGAS

Mashed Rutabagas are one of my all-time favorites. I jut love them. These were one of my stepmother Joan's best dishes. Not many people eat these, but every time I've ever served them to people who've never had them before, they go nut for them. They're absolutely awesome and Badass, and if you try them I'm sure you'll agree.

INGREDIENTS :

2 medium sized Rutabagas, peeled and cut to 1- ½" cubes
¼ Milk, ¾ stick of Butter
1/2 teaspoon Salt, ½ ground Black Pepper

Heat Milk in a small pot, then set aside. Place the Rutabagas in a large pot and fill with water and add 2 tablespoons of salt. Bring to the boil and boil until the Rutabagas are cooked through, about 15 minutes.

When the rutabagas (Yellow Turnips) are finished cooking, drain in a colander and shake off excess water.

Add the Rutabagas back to the pot they cooked in. Mash the Rutabagas with a Potato Masher. Add ½ teaspoon of Salt and ½ teaspoon Black Pepper to the Rutabagas. Add half the hot milk and mix in with a wooden spoon. Add remaining milk and half the butter and mix. Add remaining butter and mix. Your Rutabagas are ready to serve with Roast Turkey, Chicken or whatever you like. Enjoy

GREEN BEANS

INGREDIENTS :

1 pound fresh String Beans
¼ teaspoon Kosher Salt
¼ teaspoon ground Black Pepper
a pinch of Hot Red Pepper Flakes (optional)
3 Garlic cloves, peeled and sliced
10 tablespoon Olive Oil
1 tablespoon Butter

Fill a 6-quart pot with water and add 2 tablespoons Salt. Bring to the boil.

Clean the string beans by cutting off both ends, the cut beans in half. Peel and thinly slice 3 cloves of garlic.

Place string beans in the boil water and cook at a rapid boil for 4 minutes. Immediately remove from heat and drain the beans in a colander. Run cold water over the beans for two minutes, then shake off excess water.

Place olive oil in a large sauté pan and turn heat on to medium flame. When garlic starts to brown a little turn heat down to lowest flame. Add a pinch of hot red-pepper-flakes to oil. Cook for 30 seconds.

Add the String Beans, Salt & Black Pepper to pan and cook over medium heat for 4 minutes. The Green Beans are now ready to serve as a side dish to any Fish, Meat, or Poultry dish you choose.

CIOPPINO
San Francisco Style Fish Stew

Cioppino is a Fish Stew that originated in the city of San Francisco. It was first made in the late 1880's by Italian immigrant fishermen who settled in North Beach and had mostly come from the Italian Port City of Genoa. These fishermen first made the stew on their boats while out at sea. The dish later became a staple of Italian Restaurants in San Francisco of which it is still hugely popular to this day with San Franciscans and tourist alike. Ciuppino is the name of a popular fish stew from the Ligurian Coast of Italy and Genoa, while in Tuscan there is a similar stew that's called Cacciucco. No matter what you call it, this Fish Stew is as tasty as can be.

INGREDIENTS :

1 medium Onion, peeled and chopped fine
5 cloves of Garlic, peeled and minced
¼ Olive Oil
1/ teaspoon Red Pepper Flakes
1 teaspoon Sea Salt
½ teaspoon Black Pepper
1 medium Green Bell Pepper, seeded and chopped
½ cup White Wine
1 cup Clam Broth
1 ½ cups water
1 – 28 ounce can Plum Tomatoes

24 Little Neck Clams
1 pound Sea Scallops
1 pound Cod or Grouper Filet cut into 2" pieces
1 pound large Shrimp, peeled and deveined
2 Baking Potatoes, peeled and sliced
1 Bay Leaf
1 pound Jumbo Lump Crab Meat
Sliced French Bread toasted and rubbed with a raw clove of Garlic
¼ cup chopped fresh Parsley

Place the Olive Oil and Green Peppers in a large 8-quart pot and cook the Peppers on medium heat for 5 minutes. Add the onions, sprinkle with a little Salt & Black Pepper and cook on low heat for 6 minutes.

Add the wine and boil on high heat for 5 minutes.

Add the garlic & Red Pepper flakes and cook for 3 minutes on low heat. Break the tomatoes in half with your hands and add to the pot one-by-one as you break them.

Add the Clam Broth, water, Bay Leaf, Potatoes, and remaining Salt & Black Pepper and cook on medium-high heat for 25 minutes.

Add the Clams to the pot and cook on high heat until all the clams open. Remove the calms from the pot and set aside.

Add the Cod (or Grouper), the Shrimp, and Scallops and cook on medium heat until they all cook through and lose their raw color, about 5-6 minutes.

Add the Crab Meat to stew and cook on low heat for 2 minutes. Add the Clams back to the pot and cook on low heat for 1 minutes. Cover pot and let the Stew sit for 5 minutes with the cover on.

Place a piece of tasted bread on the bottom of each of 6 to 8 soup bowls and ladle Stew into each bowl, giving each person equal amounts of all the different fish and shellfish. Sprinkle with Parsley and a little Parsley and serve, as this is a most special treat.

NEW ENGLAND CLAM BAKE

A Clam Bake is one of the most festive and extravagant meals of the whole American-Table. Well extravagant and not. The extravagance is the Lobsters, along with the Shrimps, which are both higher ticket items in the realm of food. Lobster is always a treat, don't you think? I do. Many people may love and dream of having a Clam Bake, but few ever do it, as they think it is difficult and complex. It's anything but difficult, in fact it's as easy as pie. Just follow the simple recipe below and you'll be amazed it how is it is. And once you do, you're going to want to have Clam Bake Parties every year. Enjoy, it's a Clam Bake!

INGREDIENTS :

2 pounds New Potatoes, washed
2 large Onions, peeled and cut into 4 pieces
5 Celery Stalks, washed and cut in half
4 Carrots, peeled and cut into 4 pieces each
6 Garlic cloves, left unpeeled
1 can of Beer
12 cups of water
6 ears of fresh Corn, husked and broke in half
3 Bay Leaves
4 – 1 /4 pound Lobsters
1 ½ pounds Polish Kielbasa
2 dozen Little Neck Clams
2 pounds Prince Edward Island Mussels, cleaned

1 ½ pounds of Shrimp, leave in the shell
1 tablespoon salt
2 Lemons cut into 4 pieces each
3 tablespoons Butter, melted

Place the Potatoes, onions, celery, carrots, Garlic, Bay Leaves, Beer, slat, and water in a large 16-quarl pot and turn heat on to high. Let boil for 12 minutes.

Add the Lobsters, Corn, and Kielbasa and boil for 12 minutes.

Add Clams and cook for 5-6 minutes. Add Mussels and cook until the Mussels open. Add Shrimp and cook for 4 minutes. Turn heat off.

Remove all the seafood, the Corn, Carrots, and Potatoes and place onto one or two large platters. Place on the table with melted butter and Lemons and let everyone dig in!

BREAKFAST

Breakfast, they say it's the most important meal of the day, and believe it or not, it's really true. Yes, starting your day off with a good breakfast is quite important to get you going for the day. You gotta have that first cup of Joe to get you going, and you need some good solid food to fuel you with good nutrition. There are some people who skip breakfast thinking it will help them lose weight but the opposite is what happens. If you start your morning with a good breakfast you'll be less hungry during the day and eat less and take in less calories, recent medical studies have shown. And it is most important that all growing children have a good healthy breakfast each and every day. So make sure you eat a good breakfast folks.

Now on the eating, the enjoyment and pleasure of a nice hearty breakfast. Americans are known around the world to eat one of the biggest most full hearty of breakfasts. We love are Bacon, Eggs, Sausage, Home Fries, and toast with jam. Or maybe Pancakes or French Toast with or without eggs. Everyone should know how to make a good breakfast even if they can't cook that much of anything else, you should know how to make some Badass Home Fires and how to cook Scrambled and Fried Eggs and you'll be good to go. Maybe you're just starting to learn how to cook, and this is going to be your first endeavors into the kitchen.

So we've got a few good basic things to get you going, like; Home Fries, various egg preparations, French Toast, and Breakfast Burritos and Casseroles. The breakfast recipes follow and will give you a good start in the wonderful world of breakfast cookery. So do it!

Daniel Zwicke

FRENCH TOAST

When I think back to childhood and French Toast, it was always a very special treat, something fancy. Well French Toast isn't all that fancy, but as a little kid it sure seemed so, and it still does to this day as I go back there in childhood whenever I eat it. Yumm!

INGREDIENTS :

3-4 Large Eggs
6 slices White Bread
Butter, Cinnamon
¼ cup Milk
Vermont Maple Syrup (or your Choice)

Beat Milk, Eggs, and ½ teaspoon of Cinnamon in a medium sized bowl.

Heat a large frying pan on low flame.

Dip bread into beaten egg mixture 2 at a time. Add 2 tablespoons butter to pan.

Put two slices of bread or as much as will fit into the size pan you have at a time into the pan. Let cook about two minutes on each side over a low flame. Remove slices of French Toast to plates as they are finished.

Spread pats of butter over each slice of French Toast if you like. Pour Syrup over French Toast and Relish the moment!

FRIED EGGS
How to Make em ....

2 large Eggs
3 tablespoons Canola Oil
1 teaspoon Butter
Salt & Black Pepper

1 small non-stick Frying Pan and a cover

Add the Canola Oil to the Frying Pan. Turn heat on to a high flame.

Crack the 2 Eggs into a small bowl, being careful not to break the Egg Yolks. Sprinkle a little salt in the pan.

When the oil is nice and hot, carefully slide the eggs into the pan. Cook at high heat for 1 minute. Cover the pan, lower heat to low and cook egg in the cover pan for 2 ½ minutes.

Turn heat off and slide the eggs onto a plate with Home Fries or whatever your having your eggs with.

NOTE : To make *Eggs Over Easy*. After you put the eggs in pan, cook on high heat for 2 minutes. Turn the eggs over and cook on high-heat for 1 minute, and serve.

SCRAMBLED EGGS

INGREDIENTS :

3 large Eggs
¼ teaspoon each of Salt & Black Pepper
3 tablespoons Canola Oil
1 tablespoon Butter

Place the eggs in a small bowl with the Salt & Pepper and beat the eggs until they are thoroughly mixed together.

Add the Canola oil to a medium sized no-stick skillet and turn heat on high. When the oil is hot, add butter and let melt for 20 seconds. Quickly add the eggs and cook on medium-high heat and stir the eggs with a spatula or wooden spoon as you cook the eggs about 3 minutes.

The eggs are done. Put eggs on a plate, sprinkle with a little salt & pepper and serve with Home Fries, Bacon, Breakfast Sausage or whatever you like.

Some people like putting Ketchup on their Scramble Eggs, while others like some Hot Sauce, so if you're serving friends, put some Hot Sauce and Ketchup on the table for your guests and enjoy.

The DENVER OMELET

"One minute you're eating a Denver Omelet, the next minute you've got a Fuc_ing Gun in your face!"

Tim Roth at Diner in PULP FICTION

RECIPE :

2 (or 3) Extra Large or Jumbo
1/3 cup of Sliced Mushrooms
1 slice of ham cut into strips (Julienne)
¼ cup of a Red and or Green Bell Pepper diced
2 teaspoons of vegetable oil (Canola, Corn, etc.)
Salt and Ground Black Pepper
1 Scallion (Green Onion) sliced

Place a small Non-Stick Frying Pan over a burner on the stove top and turn the heat on to a medium flame. Add oil and let heat 2 minutes. Add green peppers and cook for three minutes, stirring occasionally.

Add Mushrooms and cook for three minutes. Add Scallions. Cook for three minutes.

Crack the eggs into a small bowl. Season with salt and pepper. Beat the eggs until they are one solid color of yellow.

Add ham to pan and cook for 1 minute.

Remove contents of pan to a plate or bowl on the side. Turn heat up to high. Add butter.

Heat butter for 30 seconds, then add the Beaten Eggs to pan. Cook eggs while stirring just a little bit for one minute.

Lower flame to medium and let eggs cook through and form one whole round mass the same shape as the pan.

Turn heat off. Place the reserved ham and vegetables over one side of the eggs. Fold the other side of eggs over the vegetables.

Place your Denver Omelet on a plate. Eat and Enjoy and always Abide!

NOTE: Egg White Omelets are very popular these days with people looking to cut down on the high cholesterol in an egg yolk. To make an Egg White Denver Omelet, use three eggs. Break the eggs one at a time into a bowl. After you crack one egg into the bowl, you need to remove the yolk with your hand. Do the same with the remaining 2 eggs. You will end up with a bowl of three egg whites. Add salt and pepper and beat the egg whites and proceed in the same manner as you would have with the whole eggs.

HOME FRIES

Home Fries, they're the base of many a great breakfast. Once you've got your Home Fries made all you have to do is fry up some Bacon or Breakfast Sausage, cook a couple Eggs, and you're all set to go for breakfast which they say is the most important meal of the day. Men really love to cook, and it's a good bet that when a guy is making his first forays into the kitchen and world of cooking, that Home Fries will be one of his first dishes, if not the first. So if you're one of those guys (or not) here you go, how to make Home Fries, learn this preparation and build your repertoire from here.

INGREDIENTS :

4 Idaho, Maine, or Russet Potatoes
4 tablespoons Vegetable or Olive Oil
Salt & Ground Black Pepper to taste
½ teaspoon Sweet Paprika

Place potatoes in water to cover. Add 1 tablespoon of salt. Bring to boil. Let Potatoes boil for 2 minutes. Drain the Potatoes in a colander.

Heat oil over medium flame for 1 minute. Add the potatoes to oil. Season potatoes with, Paprika and Salt & Pepper to taste. Cook over medium heat until the potatoes get a nice golden brown color and are crispy on the outside and soft inside, about for about 10 to

12 minutes stirring the Potatoes from time to time with a wooden spoon.
The Home Fries are ready to serve with eggs.

NOTE: You can add 1 medium diced or sliced onion for a little more taste. You would add the onions after the potatoes have been cooking for five minutes. You can also add some sliced Mushrooms with the onion and even some frozen Peas. Experiment and enjoy.

BREAKFAST BURRITO

INGREDIENTS :

4 large Flour Tortillas
1 small Red Bell Pepper, seeded and chopped
4 Scallions, chopped
1 medium Tomato, washed and chopped
5 ounces grated Cheddar Cheese or Monterey Jack
Salt & Black Pepper
6 tablespoons Olive Oil
1 can Black Beans
4 sprigs fresh Cilantro (optional)
6 large Eggs, beaten and season with a pinch of Salt & Pepper

Heat the beans in a small pot on low heat for 6 minutes. Warm oven to 325 degrees.

Place the Olive Oil and Bell Peppers in a large non-stick frying pan and cook on medium heat low heat for 8 minutes. Season with a pinch of Salt & Black Pepper. Add half the Scallions and cook 2 minutes on medium heat. Warm the Tortillas in 325 degree oven for 4 minutes.

Add Eggs to pan and cook on medium heat as you stir with a wooden spoon until the eggs are completely cooked through, about 3 minutes. Turn the heat off and let the eggs set in the pan.

Place a warmed tortilla down on a plate and add ¼ of the eggs onto the tortilla. Add 3 tablespoons of Black Beans on top of the eggs, then place a quarter of the Cheese on top. Top with some Scallions and Tomato and Cilantro if you're using it.

Fold the top and the bottom of the tortilla over the filling, the fold the sides to make a neatly package Burrito. Repeat to make four Breakfast Burritos. Serve and enjoy your breakfast.

BADASS BAKED BREAKFAST

INGREDIENTS :

1 pound Sausage Meat
½ pound Bacon, sliced to 1" pieces
8 slices White Bread (or any sliced bread you like)
1 ½ cups grated Cheddar Cheese
4 Scallions, chopped
8 Eggs
2 cups Milk
½ teaspoon each of Salt & Black Pepper
soft Butter to grease baking pan

Grease a 9" X 13" glass or ceramic baking pan. Line the bottom of the baking pan with the bread to cover. Heat the oven to 350 degrees.

Cook the bacon over medium heat in a large skillet until the bacon just is browned and a little crunchy, but not too crunchy or hard.

Remove Bacon with a slotted spoon and place over the top of all the bread, distributing the Bacon evenly.

Drain off all the bacon grease from the skillet and discard. Add the sausage meat to the pan and cook over medium heat until the sausage looses its raw color and is getting slightly browned. Be sure to break up the meat as you are cooking it with a wooden spoon, cooking time 7-8 minutes

Once cooked, drain the sausage in a colander and drain off all the grease from the sausage meat. Spread the sausage evenly over the bread and bacon.

Spread the Scallions over the sausage. Spread the Cheese on top of this.

Beat the eggs in a bowl. Add the Salt, Pepper, and milk and mix. Pour the eggs into the baking pan. Place the pan in the oven and bake at 350 degrees until the eggs are cooked through, about 25 minutes. Remove from oven and let sit for 8 minutes before serving.

FRIED EGGS & BOK CHOY
and Ramen Too !!!

Here is my favorite quick go to meal, one that I make all the time.
This dish is as quick and easy as it gets, real taste and cheap to boot. You need to get some nice fresh Baby Bok Choy and have eggs and Sesame Oil on hand, and you're good to go for a nice tasty little nutritious lunch that's ready in less than 10 minutes.

NOTE : I usually have this little dish for a nice healthy little light lunch, but it's great for breakfast as well and even for dinner or any time of the day.

INGREDIENTS :

1 package of Ramen Noodles
8 small whole Baby Bok Choy pieces
5 tablespoons Canola Oil (or any vegetable oil)
Salt & Black Pepper
3 tablespoons Sesame Oil
2 dashes of Maggi's Sauce (optional)
Sriracha Sauce, or other similar Red Chili Garlic Sauce

Fill a small pot with water, add 1 teaspoon of salt and bring the water to the boil. Wash the Bok Choy and split each one in half lengthwise.

Put the Bok Choy in the water and boil until the Bok Choy just start to get soft but are still very crunchy and dark green, about 2-3 minutes.

Remove Bok Choy from the pot with a slotted spoon and put in a colander. Leave all the water in the pot, and put the Ramen in. Cook the Ramen in the boiling water for 3 minutes.

Remove the Bok Choy from the colander and place on your plate.
Remove the Ramen from the water and place in the colander and let the water drain off. Place the Ramen on the plate with the Bok Choy. Season both the Bok Choy and the Ramen with a couple pinches of Salt, Black Pepper, Sesame Oil, and Sriracha or other Hot Sauce and the Maggi's Sauce if using. Mix the ramen well with the Sesame Oil and seasonings and enjoy.

The Bok Choy and Ramen are great on their own, but if you'd like to embellish the dish a bit more and with no fuss at all, up one egg and put it on the plate with the Ramen & Bok Choy and you have the most amazing little meal in minutes.

NOTE : Another alternative meal is just to fry or scramble one or two eggs and put them on the plate with the Bok Choy made the same way as above and without the Ramen. That's two quick and easy dishes for you for the price of one. Enjoy, and make it all the time as I do about 3 times a week.

THAT'S ITALIAN

Italian Food? Italian-American? Hey I'm Italian, and I feel dam lucky and proud to be so, especially when it comes to the food we eat. And the food we eat is dam good. And it's food that though originating in-and-around 1900 from Italian immigrants to America, some of the food has now become American. Yes dishes like Spaghetti with Tomato Sauce, Lasagna, Minestrone, and the much loved Spaghetti & Meatballs have become so popular in America that besides being Italian-American Cuisine dishes, they have now also become simply American. These aforementioned dishes that have been eaten by hundreds of millions of times are now so prevalent that a few of these Italian American dishes are if not completely then they are almost American. Am I making any sense here? I think you get my drift? No matter, foods like Pasta with Tomato Sauce, Chicken Parm, Spaghetti & Meatballs are loved by many, and that's all that really matters. They have become part of the American fabric and along with; Fried Chicken, Meatloaf, BBQ Chicken & Ribs these dishes of Italian-Americans are much loved and some of America's favorite foods, they're American as Apple Pie. Basta!

SPAGHETTI with TOMATO SAUCE
"Yes It's an American Classic"

Spaghetti Tomato Sauce, it's an American Classic! What? Yes, an American Classic. It's Italian yes of course, but now so prevalent in American culture that this dish from Italy brought over by Italian immigrants is now so loved and eaten by all Americans, millions of times over, the dish has become American as well. But cooking Italian Food, a good Sunday Sauce, Meatballs, or Tomato Sauce is mysterious to many Americans not of Italian origins. There's no need for the mystery and for people to be afraid of cooking pasta and a good sauce. It's quite easy, and you know you love it! And it's real cheap to boot, to feed the kid, starving artists and student alike. The recipe is below. So go for it and enjoy!

INGREDIENTS :

1/4 Olive Oil
1 small Onion, peeled and chopped fine
8 - Garlic cloves, peeled and chopped fine
2 - 28 oz. cans of Tomato Passata (Puree of Tomatoes)
1 – 28 ounce can of Crushed Tomatoes
½ teaspoon Red Pepper Flakes
3 Tablespoons Tomato Paste
1 teaspoon Oregano, 1 teaspoon Dry Basil
1/2 teaspoon Sugar
1 teaspoon Salt, 1 teaspoon Black Pepper
1 pound Imported Italian Spaghetti

Place olive oil and onions in a large pot. Turn heat on to medium, cook the onions for 5 minutes. Add the chopped Garlic and Red Pepper and cook over low heat for 4 minutes.

Drain 1 can of crushed tomatoes and reserve the liquid. Turn heat up to high, add the drained Crushed Tomatoes and cook on high heat for 4 minutes. Add the Salt & Black Pepper and continue cooking 3 minutes on low heat.

Add the reserved tomato liquid. Add remaining tomatoes, the Basil, and Oregano and cook on low heat for 55 minutes, stirring the sauce occasionally. If you see the sauce is beginning to thicken too much during the 55 minutes of cooking, add a little water to loosen it up and continue cooking.

Cook the Spaghetti in boiling salted water according to the directions on the package. When the spaghetti is done cooking, drain in a colander reserving about a ¼ cup of water to mix with the spaghetti and sauce.

Return the spaghetti back into the pot it cooked in and drizzle on a little Olive Oil. Add ¼ of the Tomato Sauce to the pot and mix. Plate the Spaghetti onto 4 separate plates or Pasta Bowls. Top each plate of Spaghetti with some more sauce on top and place the rest of the sauce in containers in the refrigerator for another days meal.

Give a plate of Spaghetti to each person having dinner and pass some grated Parmigiano or Pecorino Romano to sprinkle on the pasta. Buon Apettito!

SPAGHETTI MEATBALLS

Spaghetti & Meatballs, who doesn't love them? Not many I tell you. They're in the Top 50 of America's Favorite Dishes, so here they are, in this book of America's favorite most BadAss Food, Spaghetti & Meatballs are right up there with Fried Chicken, Meatloaf, Hamburgers, Tacos, and our beloved BBQ Ribs. Go for it, and Eat Like an Italian. Mangia Bene!

INGREDIENTS :

1 pound Ground Beef
1 pound Ground Pork
2 cloves Garlic, minced fine
2 Eggs
½ cup freshly grated Pecorino Romano Cheese
1/4 chopped Italian Flat Leaf Parsley
Salt and Black Pepper to taste
1cup stale Italian bread, crumbled
1 cup of Milk or Water to soak stale bread in
olive oil for cooking

Mix all ingredients except olive oil in a large bowl. Shape the meat into Meatballs of whatever size you prefer; small, medium, or large.

Fry Meatballs in olive oil over a medium heat until they are nicely browned.

Finish cooking in *Sauce (recipe follows).*

The SAUCE

INGREDIENTS :

1/4 Olive Oil
1 Large Onion chopped fine
3 Garlic cloves, peeled and chopped fine
4 - 28 oz. cans Tomatoes (crush 3 cans of tomatoes and leave 1 can of tomatoes whole) Use all the watery juice in sauce. Do not throw away
3 Tablespoons Tomato Paste
1 teaspoon Oregano
1 teaspoon Dry Basil
1/2 teaspoon Sugar
1 teaspoon Salt
1 teaspoon Black Pepper

Place olive oil and onions in a large pot. Turn heat on to medium, cook for 3 minutes. Lower heat to low, cook 3 minutes.

Add chopped Garlic. Cook over low heat for 4 minutes.

Drain 1 can of whole tomatoes that you do not chop. Add whole tomatoes to pot, reserving the watery juice, which you add after all tomatoes have been added. Turn heat up to high and cook tomatoes. Break up tomatoes with wooden spoon. Cook tomatoes on high heat for 3-4 minutes.

Add all remaining ingredients. Cook over high heat until sauce starts bubbling. Lower heat to very low and cook over low heat for 1 hour.
After the sauce has been cooking for a half hour, start making the Meatballs.

Once the Meatballs have been shaped and browned, add the browned Meatballs into the Tomato Sauce that has been cooking for 1 hour.

Continue cooking the Sauce over low heat with the Meatballs for about 35 minutes.

Cook one pound of Spaghetti, Ronzoni or Imported Spaghetti from Italy. Figure on 1 pound for every 3 or 4 people. Use 1 pound for 3 people if you have hungry eaters who want seconds. Cook Spaghetti according to directions on package. Make sure the water is seasoned with salt and always at a rapid boil or it will become gummy.

When Spaghetti is finished cooking, drain in a colander, reserving about ¼ cup of the pasta cooking water. Add the drained Spaghetti back into the pot it cooked in. Add some of the "Sauce" to the Spaghetti and mix. Sprinkle a little Olive Oil over the Spaghetti and mix again.

Portion out Spaghetti onto plates or pasta bowls. Top the Spaghetti with some more Sauce. Add 2 or 3 Meatballs to each plate and serve to your guests.

BADASS PORCHETTA

Porchetta is one of the most Badass dishes the World has ever known. As they say down South, "They're so Dam Good, you'll wanna Slap Your Mamma." And dam it doesn't get better than that. Porchetta, so what is it you want to know? Well I guess the best way to describe it to many American's is that it's the Italian Version of Barbecued Pork and a dam good one at that. Well all different types of American Barbecued Pork have all different types of seasonings and that's the main difference in the seasoning. In America Pit Masters have their own Secret Rubs to season the meat with, then slow cook it until its succulently tender and delicious as can be. Whereas American Barbecue Pork meat might have a dry-rub seasoning of things like; Cayenne Pepper, Paprika, Garlic Powder, Sugar, and Cumin, the Italian Prochetta is seasoned with; Garlic, Fennel, Rosemary, Black Pepper, and Sage. The American seasonings of the pork will vary from cook to cook, whereas the Italian Porchetta usually sticks to a standard seasoning recipe more or less.

So if you're a lover of Roast Pork and Barbecue and you've never had Porchetta before, do like millions of Italians do every year and give this one a whirl, I guarantee your gonna love it. Basta!

INGREDIENTS For BADASS PORCHETTA :

¼ cup Olive Oil
¼ cup Fennel Fronds
7 sprigs Rosemary, leaves removed from stems
8 Sage leaves, chopped
6 cloves Garlic, Peeled
1 teaspoon Fennel Seeds
zest of one Lemon
1 ½ teaspoons Kosher Salt
¾ teaspoons Black Pepper
½ teaspoon Red Pepper Flakes
1 whole Pork Shoulder with skin on (about 6-7 pounds)
2 large Onions, peeled and sliced thickly

Put first 10 ingredients in a food processer and pulse until all are thoroughly mixed into a paste, about 2 minutes.

Place the onions in a large baking pan and drizzle a little Olive Oil over the onions. Rub the paste completely all over the pork shoulder. Cover with plastic wrap in put in the refrigerator to marinate for 3-4 hours or over night.

Remove the Pork Shoulder from the refrigerator at least 1 hour before putting in the oven. Heat oven to 400 degrees 15 minutes before you will be putting the pork in.

Roast the Pork for 30 minutes at 400 degrees. Lower the oven to 350 degrees and roast the pork until done, about 2 hours and 45 minutes to 3 hours, until a meat thermometer stuck into the Pork reads 175 degrees.

Remove from oven and let rest 15 minutes before serving. Cut the Porchetta into thick slices and serve with Roast Potatoes or whatever vegetable you like, or of course the Porchetta makes one of the World's Great Sandwiches, just slice some and put onto good Italian Bread or Hero Rolls, and you're gonna go out of your mind at the *other-worldly* taste of it all.

GENERAL TSO'S CHICKEN

General Tso's Chicken has become a great favorite of many American's, it not the # 1 favorite Chinese dish of all. Most people would never think of making it themselves, but getting it from their local Chinese Restaurant, and we understand that. But there are those of us who love to cook and are always looking to try new recipes. If you're one of those people, well here you go, here's a tasty recipe for this famous Chinese dish that Americans love so much, and it's not that hard to do. Make it a couple times and you'll become a pro, and you can impress your friends with you ability to make what? General Tso's Chicken of course! Go for it!

INGREDIENTS :

1 pound of Boneless Skinless Chicken Breasts
1 Egg White
½ teaspoon Salt
2 tablespoons Dark Soy Sauce
3 tablespoons Dry Sherry
½ cup Corn Starch
6 tablespoons Canola Oil
3 slices of fresh Ginger, minced
2 garlic cloves, peeled and minced
4 Dry Chilies, de-seeded
4 Scallions, sliced to ½" pieces

Canola Oil for Frying

SAUCE :

2 ½ tablespoons Rice Wine Vinegar
4 tablespoons Soy Sauce
2 tablespoons Housin Sauce
¼ cup Water
Dry Sherry
Cornstarch

Mix these ingredients for the sauce together in a bowl and set aside. Cut chicken into 1-inch pieces.

Place the Soy Sauce from top list, Salt, and Dry Sherry in a bowl and mix. And the chicken and mix. Let marinate for 15 minutes.

Heat 3 cups of Canola oil in a pot to fry the chicken in.

Remove the chicken from the marinade and let marinade drain off in a colander or wire strainer. Add the chicken to the cornstarch and mix. Shake off excess cornstarch from the chicken and put in the pot with oil to fry.

Fry chicken until it turns light brown, about 3-4 minutes. Add the 6 tablespoons Canola Oil to a Wok or large skillet and turn heat on to medium-high. Add the Garlic, Ginger, and Chilies and cook for 3 minutes.

Pour the sauce in the Wok (pan) and cook until the sauce thickens Add the chicken to the sauce and cook two minutes on low heat. Add the Scallions and cook for 30 seconds more. The Chicken is done. Serve with boil rice. Enjoy.

STEAK DIANE

INGREDIENTS :

4 Filet Mignon Steaks, cut 2 1/2 " thick
2 tablespoons Canola Oil
2 tablespoons Butter
Garlic
1 Shallot, peeled and
6 ounces Button Mushrooms, sliced
¼ cup Chicken Stock
¼ cup Cognac or French Brandy
¼ cup Heavy Cream, 1 tablespoon Worcestershire Sauce
1 tablespoon Dijon Mustard
1/2 teaspoon each of Kosher Salt & Black Pepper
6 tablespoons fresh chopped Parsley
3 tablespoons chopped Chives
Season both sides of the Steaks liberally with Salt & Black Pepper. Place Canola Oil in a medium skillet and turn heat on to high. Place the steaks in the pan and cook 5 minutes on the first side at high heat. Turn the steak over and cook to medium-rare, about 4 – 5 minutes.

Remove steaks from pan and set aside on a plate covered with aluminum foil to keep steaks warm. Add Butter and Mushrooms and season mushrooms with a little salt & Pepper. Cook the mushrooms on high heat for 2 minutes while stirring. Add the Shallots and Garlic and cook on low heat for 3 minutes.

Add the Cognac and let cook on high heat. Add chicken stock and Worcestershire Sauce cook on medium heat for 4 minutes.

Add Cream and cook on high heat until the Cream starts to thickens, about 4 minutes.

Turn the heat off, add the Parsley and Mustard to pan and mix.

Place each Filet Mignon on a plate. Divide the sauce over the four Steaks, and top each Filet of Beef with chopped Chives and serve.

Steak Diane goes well with Mashed Potatoes or Buttered Carrots on the side.

CHICKEN in a POT
Poulet au Pot

It was King Henri IV of France who said those famous words "A Chicken in Every Pot," of his wish that the peasant folks of France would all be able to have Chicken for dinner at least once a week on Sunday. Almost 300 years later American President Hoover uttered these same words of a Chicken in Every Pot, and the rest is history. Anyway, Chicken in a Pot, most would think the dish isn't very appetizing, and I wouldn't have myself as well if I hadn't eaten the dish myself. Chicken in a Pot is surprisingly tasty cooked in this manner, and you've got the Chicken, Carrots, and Potatoes that pick up the Chicken flavor. You sprinkle salt and pepper over everything and the Horseradish Sauce on the Chicken taste real good and pulls everything together. Enjoy this one, you'll be surprised how much you do. I guarantee!

INGREDIENTS :

1 – whole 3 to 3 ½ pound Chicken
4 Carrots, peeled and cut into 6 pieces each
2 Celery Stalks, washed and cut into 3 pieces each
2 Baking Potatoes, peeled and cut into 8 pieces each
6 cloves Garlic left whole
½ teaspoon Kosher Salt, 1 Bay Leaf
10 whole Black Peppercorns
5 teaspoons prepared Horseradish
5 tablespoons Mayonnaise

¼ cup fresh chopped parsley

Place the Chicken and all the ingredients except for the horseradish, parsley, and mayonnaise in a medium sized pot and fill with water to come over the chicken by 2 inches.

Turn the heat on and bring to the boil. Lower the heat so the liquid is at a low-medium simmer and cook the chicken for 1 hour and 20 minutes. Turn the heat off and cover the pan and let the chicken sit in its broth for 15 minutes.

Remove chicken from the pot and let cool for 5 minutes.

In a small bowl, mix the Mayonnaise with the Horseradish for the sauce.

Break the Chicken into 4 quarters, 2 Legs &Thighs together and two Breasts with wings and place a quarter chicken on each plate with equal amounts of Carrots and Potatoes on each plate. Sprinkle with chopped Parsley and serve the Horseradish Sauce, Black Pepper and Kosher Salt on the side. Enjoy, this dish is a lot tastier than most people think.

LOBSTER NEWBURG

INGREDIENTS :

2 – 1 ¼ pound Lobsters
5 tablespoons Cream Sherry
½ teaspoon Kosher Salt
1 Shallot, peeled and minced
1 stalk of Celery, washed and minced
2 tablespoons Butter, 1 ½ cups Heavy Cream
1 tablespoon Paprika, ¼ teaspoon ground Nutmeg

Fill a large 12-quart pot with water and bring to the boil. Add Lobsters and cook at the boil for 10 minutes. Turn off heat. Remove lobsters from water and set aside to cook.

After the lobsters have cooled remove all the meat from the shells and cut into large pieces about 2 ½" thick.

Put butter in a pan with the Celery and Shallots and cook on medium heat for 5 minutes. Add Sherry and cook on high heat until sherry is reduced by half its original volume, about four minutes.

Add the cream, Salt, Paprika, and Nutmeg to the pan and cook on medium heat until the cream starts to thicken, about 5-6 minutes. Add the Lobster Meat to the pan, lower heat and cook to heat the lobster on a low flame, about 4 minutes. Turn heat off, the lobster is ready to serve. Serve over toast rounds or toast triangles, a smaller portion as an appetizer or large portion of lobster for a main-course.

BADASS GOULASH

INGREDIENTS :

2 ½ pounds Beef Chuck (or Beef Shank) cut into 2"
pieces
12 tablespoons Olive Oil (or any vegetable oil)
2 large Onion, peeled and sliced
4 cloves Garlic, peeled and sliced
5 Carrots, peeled and cut into 2 " pieces
2 Baking Potatoes, peeled and cut into 2" cubes
1 Bay Leaf
1 tablespoon Caraway Seeds
½ teaspoon Salt
2 Tablespoons Sweet Paprika
½ teaspoon Black Pepper
¾ cup dry white wine
2 tablespoons Baslamic Vinegar
3 tablespoons Tomato Paste
1 ½ tablespoons dry Marjoram
 2 – 14 ounce cans Chicken Broth
6 tablespoons fresh chopped Parsley

Cut the Beef into 2" cubes and season with Salt &
Black Pepper. Put half the oil in a large 8-quart pot and
turn the heat on high. Add half the Beef and cook until
all the beef is nice and brown on all side, about 8-9
minutes. Remove the browned beef from pan and set
aside.

Add remaining beef to pot and cook on high heat the same as the first batch of beef. Remove from pot and set aside.

Add the Wine & Vinegar to pot and cook on high heat until the wine is reduce to half its original volume. Pour the wine out of pot and set aside.

Add remaining oil and the onions to the pot and cook on low heat for 10 minutes. Add the Paprika, Salt, Black Pepper, and Garlic to the pan and cook on low heat for 3 minutes.

Add the Tomato Paste, the Wine, Chicken Broth and the Beef back to the pot. Add all the remaining ingredients, except the Egg Noodles and Parsley to the pot and bring contents to the boil. Once the liquid comes to the boil, lower the heat to a medium simmer and cook until the Beef is tender, about 1 hour and 30 minutes. The Goulash is done.

Cook the Egg Noodles according the directions on the package. Remove noodles from the pot and drain in a colander. Shake off excess water and put noodles bake in the pot they cooked in and add 1 ½ tablespoons of butter and mix.

Divide the Egg Noodles evenly amongst 4 plates. Top the noodles with the Goulash, sprinkle chopped Parsley on top and enjoy the fruits of your labors. You deserve it.

Daniel Zwicke

BEST CHOCOLATE CHIP COOKIES EVER

Chocolate Chip Cookies, I'd wager to say might very well be America's favorite sweet treat of all. What's more popular, can anyone tell me? I think probably nothing, and I do know that they are my personal favorite. An if they're not # 1 in popularity, I'm certain they're somewhere in the Top 5, wouldn't you agree? No, matter, most of us Love them to death! How bout you?

INGREDIENTS :

1 ½ cups All-Purpose Flour
½ teaspoon Baking Soda
3 ounces Butter (1 stick)
½ cup Sugar
½ cup Light Brown Sugar
¼ teaspoon Salt
1 Egg
1 teaspoon Vanilla Extract
8 ounce Dark Chocolate Chips

Sift flour and baking soda together and set aside.

Place butter in a mixing bowl and cream with an Electric Mixer. Add the Sugar, the Brown Sugar, and Salt and continue mixing.

Add the Egg and Vanilla and mix at low speed for 1 minutes.

Add half the flow and beat at slow speed for 30 seconds. Add remaining four and beat at low speed until flour is totally mixed in.

Add the Chocolate Chips and mix with a rubber spatula or wooden spoon. Heat oven to 350 degrees.

Grease to cookie sheets with butter. Take tablespoons of the dough and drop onto the cookie sheets leaving until all the dough is gone. Make sure to leave space in-between the dough to expand.

OREO CHEESECAKE

INGREDIENTS :

24 Oreo Cookies
3 ½ tablespoons melted Butter, 3 Eggs
3 – 10 0z. Packages of Cream Cheese, at room temperature
¾ cup granulated Sugar, 1 teaspoon Vanilla Extract

Put 16 Oreos in a large plastic bag and mash with a rolling pin or back of a pan to break-up and crush the cookies. Place these crumbled Oreos in a bowl with the melted butter and mix.

Press the crumbled Oreos in to the bottom of a 9" spring-form pan.

Place Cream Cheese and Sugar in a glass bowl and mix with an electric mixer until well blended. Add eggs one at a time and mix. Add Vanilla and mix.

Crush remaining cookies. Add half of these cookies to the cream cheese mixture and mix by hand with a wooden spoon or spatula.

Put the cream cheese mixture into the pan and top with remaining crushed Oreos. Bake the cheesecake at 350 degrees for 50-55 minutes.

Remove from the oven and let cool 30 minutes at room temperature. Place in the refrigerator and cool at least 3 hours before serving.

BANANA'S FOSTER

Bananas Foster is a fabulous dessert that's sure to please just about anyone. It's an elegant dessert that's easy to make and sure to impress. Bananas Foster is the most famously supreme dessert of the great culinary city of New Orleans. It was invented by Chef Paul Blange at Brennan's Restaurant in 1951, and has been going strong ever since. It's served at all the great New Orleans restaurants like; Arnaud's, Commander's Palace, Antoine's, and Galatoire's, and now you can serve it at home. Make it for your friends and I guarantee they will be very impressed, enjoy.

INGREDIENTS :

½ stick Butter, 1 cup Brown Sugar
½ teaspoon Cinnamon
¼ cup Banana Liqueur
4 Bananas, cut in half lengthwise, the in-half crosswise
½ cup Dark Rum

Place the Butter, Brown Sugar, and Cinnamon in a medium sized skillet. Turn on a low flame and cook while stirring with a wooden spoon until the sugar dissolves.

Add Banana Liqueur and cook one minute on low heat. Add the Bananas. Cook 2 minutes on low heat.

Add the Rum and cook 1 minute. Tip the pan so the fire from flame will ignite the Rum. Cook until flame dies out.

Place one scoop each of Vanilla Ice Cream in 4 small bowls. Place 4 pieces of Banana around the Ice Cream, and cover the ice cream with equal portions of the sauce. Serve immediately.

TENDING THE BAR

OK, so you've gone through the book and cooked at least a few dishes in the book. Did you try the Fried Chicken, cook a Perfect Steak, make some Cowboy Chili, Badass BBQ Sauce, and Gumbo? Well you know how to cook a few dishes. Maybe you know a lot, and it's not your first day at the Rodeo. How bought Cocktails? Do you know how to make any? Well if you don't, isn't it a good idea you knew one or two, 3 or 4? The basics. Hell Yeah it is! And it's a dam good idea at that. So I've put a little something here for you to get started. Hey, you're having a dinner party, so why not make some cocktails for your friends to start thing off, which is just adding one more wonderfully Badass dimension to your already Badass dinner party. Deviled Eggs or Devils on Horseback would make some great horse d'oeuvres to go along with the cocktails. Guacamole is another great item as well.

So, anyway, we've got a few cocktails here to get you started. If you want more, then just get yourself one of the many good bartending books out there, there's a whole mess of them. This is a cookbook after all. I thought I'd throw in a few recipes for some of America's favorite cocktails, but that's it. Anyway, I hope you enjoy the few I've put down here.

HOW to MAKE a MARTINI

The 3 Martini was *de Rigeur* during 1950's and 60's American life. That's how popular this classic American Cocktail was, and it's popularity has not waned. James Bond likes his "Shaken, Not Stirred." How do you think you might like yours? The classic recipe is below, however there are variations on the theme, so experiment and have fun and always enjoy.

Ingredients:

4 ounces of Gin (Bombay, Tanqueray, Gordon's or other)
2 teaspoons Dry Vermouth
1 – 3 Martini Olives (large Green Olives stuffed with Pimento)
Ice

Fill a Martini Glass with ice and let it chill for at least 5 minutes.

Fill a cocktail shaker with ice cubes. Add the Gin and the Dry Vermouth, cover the shaker with the top and shake vigorously for 2 minutes.

Remove the ice from the martini Glass. Add an Olive or 2 or three to the glass. Pour the Gin & Vermouth out of the shaker, straining it to leave the ice behind, and serve.

NOTE : to make a Vodka Martini, use Vodka instead of Gin. Make sure that you get the best quality gin or Vodka for your Martini and not one of those cheap budget brands, if you want to make the best Martini possible.

Daniel Zwicke

THE MANHATTAN COCKTAIL

The Manhattan Cocktail is one of the World's most classic cocktails and is made with blended Rye Whiskey, Sweet Vermouth and Bitters and garnish with a Maraschino Cherry or Lemon Twist.

INGREDIENTS:

3 ounces Rye Whiskey (Seagrams 7, Canadian Club, Bullet)
1 ounce Sweet Vermouth
1 Maraschino Cherry
2 dashes of Angostura Bitters
Ice
1 Cocktail Glass

Place the Rye Whiskey and Sweet Vermouth in a Cocktail Shaker that's filled with ice. Shake well for 1 ½ minutes.

Place a Maraschino Cherry in the glass and strain the Whiskey / Sweet Vermouth into the glass, and serve immediately.

THE OLD FASHION COCKTAIL

The Old Fashion is considered one of the greatest cocktails ever invented, and that's something I would agree to. It's one of my favorites, along with the Negroni and Mojito cocktails are my drinks of choice. Though an old classic cocktail, Old Fashion's have become extremely popular in the last 5 years or so. Though I've been drinking them for years and it's the only thing I like to drink whenever I'm down in the Big Easy, New Orleans, even though the Sazerac is the official cocktail of New Orleans, I'd rather have an Old Fashion, and I'm not the only one. Old Fashion Cocktails are one of the favored drinks of New Orleans. However, whenever I'm at one of my favorite bars in the world down in the Big Easy, and I'm at Napoleon House in the French Quarter, I always have one or two Pimm's Cups the house cocktail and the best place to have that cocktail in America. If you're ever in New Orleans, you do the same.

Ingredients :

3 ounces Whiskey of your choice (Bourbon or Rye)
1 wedge of a fresh Orange slice
1 Maraschino Cherry
5 dashes of Angostura Bitters
Ice
1 Rock Glass

Place the Orange, Sugar, Cherry in the bottom of your rock glass. Shake on 5 dashes of Bitters onto the Orange. Now you are going to do what is called muddling, which is crushing the Orange and Cherry together with the sugar and bitters.

Once you have muddle the orange and cherry, fill the glass with ice, then fill the glass almost to the top with Whiskey and stir.

Your Old fashion is ready, drink and enjoy.

THE NEGRONI

As I've already stated, the Negroni along with the Mojito and the Old Fashion are my three favorite cocktails and ones I drink most. Every now and then I might get a hankering for a gin & Tonic made with Bombay Gin, but more often then not it's an old Fashion or Negroni with the Mojito coming in third. Negroni have just recently become a very popular cocktail in the US, but I've been drinking these puppy's since my first trip to Italy way back in 1985, when I had my first one a one of the Grande Caffes in the Eternal City of Rome. There was nothing like it and often think of that first Negroni every time a have another.

Basic Recipe:

1 ounce Campari
1 ounce Sweet Vermouth
1 ounce Gin
Ice
Orange

Fill a Rocks-Glass or Highball Glass with Ice.

Add Campari, Sweet Vermouth, and Gin.

Stir ingredients. Garnish with a piece of Orange Peel or slice of Orange.

Note: Orsen Wells after discovering the Negroni while writing a screenplay in Rome, wrote in a correspondence back home that he had discovered a delightful Italian Cocktail, "The Negroni." Welles stated, *"It is made of Bitter Campari which is good for the liver, and of Gin which is bad. The two balance each other out."*

APEROL SPRTIZ

No it's not a classic American Cocktail, but the way it's going, it may very well be one day. The Aperol Spritz is by far Italy's new favorite cocktail, even beating out the older and more classic Negroni. If you've been to Italy lately, especially on the Amalfi Coast you've no doubt seen these cocktail on tables in every restaurant, bar and caffe around. They're hugely popular and Americans visiting Italy have taken quite well to them and drink them quite a bit at home, thus making the Aperol Spritz one America's new favorite cocktails. It's quite refreshing and a great drink to have if you want a cocktail but something that's not that strong, an Aperol Spritz sure fits the bill.

Ingredients :

3 ounces Prosecco
2 ounces Aperol
1 ounce Club Soda
1 Orange Slice
Ice

Fill a large wine glass with ice. Add the Orange Slice. Add the Prosecco and Aperol and stir. Add the club soda and drink up.

The MARGARITA

Who doesn't love a good Margarita? Well many I guess, but I bet there are more who love it then not. It's one of America's favorite cocktails, and we think you should know how to make one, so here you go.

Ingredients :

2 ounces Tequila (Jose Cuervo, Patron or other)
1 ounces Triple Sec or Cointreau
1 ounce Lime Juice (fresh Lime Juice or Roses Lime Juice)
1 wedge or slice of Lime
Ice
1 Cocktail Glass

Fill a cocktail shaker with ice. Add the Tequila, Triple Sec (or Cointreau) and Lime Juice in the shaker. Cover the shaker with the top and shake for 1-2 minutes.

Strain the contents into your cocktail glass. Garnish the rim of the glass with the slice of Lime and serve.

IN CLOSING

Well, I sure do hope you like this book. There's lots of great recipes in, and a bit of good advice as well. The recipes here within are what I believe are the best loved and most popular dishes in all of America. Things like Fried Chicken, BBQ Spare Ribs, Chili, Burgers, and such are the most revered of all and on the top of the list of what Americans really go nuts for. Certain ethnic dishes have almost it seems have become American as Apple Pie. Thins like Tacos, Burritos, Spaghetti & Meatballs, and General Tso's Chicken though originating in other countries like Italy, China, Mexico, or wherever and now part of every day American life and what Americans love to eat, that it seems many ethnic dishes are American.

I tried giving a little advice as to saving money, and lots of it by cooking at home. You can literally save thousands of dollars a year, each and every year simply by cooking at home a certain amount of time during the year. It doesn't mean that you can't eat out, just that maybe you might want to cut down on the amount of eating out or getting take-out, saving lots of money for other necessities of life like; money to go towards your vacation, to buy Christmas Presents, put in the bank or whatever, it's extra cash to do with what you want. You'll learn how to make new dishes, have family meals at home, thus strengthening the family unit and making lifetime memories and good times.

You'll learn how to cook for friends, to throw little dinner parties, picnics, barbecues and what not. These are all good things and only add to the betterment of a happier life for you and yours. So again my friends, thanks for getting this book. I do hope you enjoyed and will use this book many times over the years. It's the Badass Cookbook *and the Badass equals extra good.*

Thanks Again,

Daniel

Daniel Zwicke

by The Same Author

SUNDAY SAUCE
When Italian-Americans Cook

THE FEAST of THE 7 FISH
Italian Christmas

SEGRETO ITALIANO
Secret Italian Recipes

GRANDMA BELLINO COOKBOOK
Recipes From My Sicilian Grandmother

La TAVOLA
*Italian New Yorkers Adventures
of The Table*

RAGU BOLOGNESE COOKBOOK

GOT ANY KAHLUA ?
aka The BIG LEBOWSKI COOKBOOK

Daniel Zwicke

CPSIA information can be obtained
at www.ICGtesting.com
Printed in the USA
BVOW06s1831130817
491963BV00009B/66/P